The

SisterWitch

Conspiracy

To Bernice,

With memories
of the thrilling
music we played
together.

Your sister,
Sonia

Other Titles by Sonia Johnson

From Housewife to Heretic

Going Out of Our Minds: The Metaphysics of Liberation

Wildfire: Igniting the She/Volution

The Ship that Sailed into the Living Room: Sex and Intimacy Reconsidered

Out of This World: A True-Life Adventure (with Jade DeForest)

Inquiries may be sent to soniajohnson3@gmail.com.

Back cover photograph by Gail Bryan © 2010; all rights reserved
Cover design by Rand Hall

Acknowledgements

As I wrote this book, I became aware once again of how indebted I am to the dozens of feminists whose thinking over many years has contributed to, overlapped, and coincided with my own until, quite honestly, I often cannot tell whose is specifically whose anymore. If I have not given credit where credit is due, I have not done it knowingly, and will make what reparations I can.

However, at the outset I want to recognize Sally Tatnall and Phyllis Balzerzak for their work of the late 1980's and early 1990's on stimulus/response and sadomasochism. Their thinking crystallized for all time my understanding of hierarchy, underlies much of Chapters 3 and 14, and is an invisible ideological aura permeating this book. For more about them, see the index of my book, *The Ship that Sailed Into the Living Room: Sex and Intimacy Reconsidered*.

I am also deeply and particularly indebted to Mary Daly for her theory of patriarchal reversal. Almost every day of my life since I read *Gyn/Ecology* decades ago, this idea has clarified reality for me more than any other of her fine gifts. It has become so basic to my thinking that, as I reread this book, I hear echoes of it throughout.

Now Fortune has smiled on me again, this time in the guise of talented and generous women who, though they do not necessarily agree with my opinions, helped me put this book together. My thanks to Rand Hall, cover designer; Gail Bryan, photographer; Ann Marevis, copy editor and proofreader; deJoly LaBrier, computer consultant; Gale Fairchild and Karen Foss, readers; and Jade Deforest, publicist, general advisor, lover and friend *extraordinaire*.

TO THE MEMORY OF

Mary Daly
(1928-2010)

Contents

A Few Words Before I Begin xi

Preface xiii

❦ ❦ ❦

PART I: THE SISTERWITCH LEGACY

Chapter 1: Sisterhood: Echoes of The SisterWitch
Connection...1

Chapter 2: Jade's Story 15

Chapter 3: Patriarchy and Maleness 25

❦ ❦ ❦

PART II: THE SISTERWITCH WAY

Chapter 4: Timelessness: The SisterWitch Ambience........39

Chapter 5: The SisterWitch Reality 45

Chapter 6: The SisterWitch World of Being.....................63

❦ ❦ ❦

PART III: MALENESS AND THE ERASURE OF THE SISTERWITCH UNIVERSE

Chapter 7: The Rule of the Retrograde..............................75

Chapter 8: The Good Man 89

Chapter 9: Telling the Truth...97

❦ ❦ ❦

PART IV: BEING THERE

Chapter 10: Home Again...119

Chapter 11: Parthenogenesis, Babies, and Motherhood...125

Chapter 12: Reconsidering Chapter 11 133

Chapter 13: New Friends 143

Chapter 14: Intimacy, the SisterWitch Essence 147

PART V: THE SISTERWITCH CONSPIRACY

Chapter 15: The SisterWitch Promise.............................173
Chapter 16: Our Planet, Ourselves 181
Chapter 17: Restoring the Sisterhood, Recovering
    the Power..
                                                        193
Chapter 18: The Embrace..215

About the Author...219

A Few Words Before I Begin

I remember being on an airplane in the late 1980's struggling against an almost overwhelming despair. I had finally admitted to myself that as long as men were on the planet, neither peace nor justice would ever be possible. Since there always *had* been men (hadn't there?) and since there always *would* be men (wouldn't there?), there was no hope for a better world. I wished fervently that the plane would fall out of the sky right then and spare me the agony of trying to live for the rest of my life in such hopelessness.

Looking back, I'm surprised at how thoughtlessly I accepted the assumption that men had always existed and always would. I'm surprised at how, despite having spent years identifying the false assumptions that make patriarchy possible, on the plane that day I automatically accepted perhaps the single most crucial lie of them all: that men and women share the same origins and the same destiny.

Not as an excuse for this lapse but as an explanation: the assumptions underlying the male paradigm that I overlooked have become such givens that they are as invisible as the air we breathe. But more than this. The truths that, if remembered, could have seriously disempowered patriarchy have been buried under so many layers of falsehood by this time that they are not only almost completely lost to us, but are also nearly unthinkable and unimaginable, and if stumbled upon, seemingly so ludicrous and heretical as to appear insane.

But it is patriarchy itself that is insane; anything we can imagine outside it is greatest sanity.

Fortunately, the plane did not fall out of the sky that day. Instead, I began a journey toward that sanity, a journey in a direction that restored my hope and my passion for life.

This book is part of that journey. It is a book about gender—a hidden, profoundly taboo gender. To be more exact, it is about a *species* of beings whose existence and nature have been deliberately erased from memory. But not entirely. Now at the end of patriarchy, these memories are becoming increasingly irrepressible and beginning to tell us an amazing story.

This is a book also about the most thrilling time in men's history, a time foretold for centuries by the women of ancient peoples and now almost upon us. I have thought about little else for twenty years. To you who have chosen to join me in these pages, I offer some of these thoughts. Because they've been on my mind, I'm pretty sure they've been on yours, too, and perhaps on the minds of even more women than we dare hope. Whether we agree on anything is not important; what *is* important is that we feel the same urgency to discover and prepare to do whatever it is that each of us is here now to do.

Though you are in my mind as I write, I also write for myself—to remember what I believe, what I value, what I most powerfully know. I write to contradict my profound brainwashing and to go out of my patriarchal mind, to remember femaleness, to invent it when memory fails, to delight in my passion for the lost world that is its essence. I write to create a haven of spiritual coherence for myself in the vast dislocation and confusion we now inhabit between worlds.

Above all, I write to let my love for all things female, including your longing self and mine, engulf me and restore my soul.

❧ ❧ ❧

Preface

Not long after males appeared in our world, our attempts to mitigate their disastrous effects required that we meet together often, secretly and for a purpose—though both "secrecy" and "purpose" were new and disturbing modes of being to us. Nevertheless, these gatherings proved necessary and we continued them from life to life.

Down through the centuries, however, as our hurt and anger grew, so did our rebelliousness, and sometimes when it erupted in dangerous ways—perhaps as carelessness about where and when we flew—men hunted us down and killed us. Fear of discovery finally taught us wisdom enough to keep our treason hidden; at heart, though, we remained rebels, still coming together in deepest secrecy to share what we knew about our original world and selves, to remember together what we had been and who we most amazingly still were.

We taught our daughters and our female students—under the guise of instructing them in music, or housewifery, or religion—about a marvelous lost world and a Sisterhood powerful beyond imagining. We developed veiled ways of communicating with one another even in men's presence, and—more carefully now, out of men's sight—we flew, healed one another, made miracles.

In this way—through covens, goddess circles, nunneries, prayer groups, sewing circles—down to the Burning Times of men's Renaissance, our resistance movement kept our passion for femaleness alive. Although the SisterWitch Conspiracy was then driven violently and deeply underground, the memory of it has been a never-failing beacon to women, for centuries connecting those of us with like minds in every hamlet and town on this planet.

What did we tell one another in those secret gatherings? What knowledge—so subversive to patriarchy that it meant death to us when discovered—did we have the courage to believe, pass along to other women, and promise never to forget?

Who were we?

Who *are* we?

❧ ❧ ❧

PART I

The SisterWitch Legacy

Chapter 1

Sisterhood: Echoes of The SisterWitch Connection

Some old friends are sitting around the kitchen table after dinner one evening, reminiscing about their activist days, laughing, having another slice of cake, another cup of cider.

Saralena wipes her mouth, lays her napkin down and, looking up at the familiar faces in the soft lamplight, says contentedly, "This has been great, the five of us together again. Almost like being back in the day—the energy of it, the feeling of community . . ."

Elinor nods. "I still miss that time, you know. After all these years. The crazy hopefulness of it, the wild discussions and arguments, our brilliant actions."

"Works of art—actually works of *genius*—our civil disobedience!" Saralena interjects.

"We gave it everything we had," Mattie says. "Sometimes I still can't believe we weren't successful."

Elinor turns to her. "Well," she replies, "there are those who say we *were* successful. According to them, the Women's Movement opened lots of doors that had been closed to women before."

"But what do *you* say, Elinor?" Mattie asks.

Elinor shrugs. "There's some truth to it. It's just, well . . . it seems . . . ," she struggles for words.

". . . so little compared with the dream?" Mattie offers.

"Yes, something like that," Elinor says. "The doors that opened, opened into such small spaces."

"Such bo-o-o-ring spaces!" Mattie adds.

"Boring, yeah, but also as unprincipled as what went before—instead of revealing something *else*, some larger, more moral possibility." Elinor looks away, adds softly, "Something more beautiful."

"They all just opened into ugly old patriarchy again," Mattie agrees. "And we'd been there, done that."

She stops a moment, then ventures, "But you know, even if we'd ratified the Equal Rights Amendment, I think in time we'd have been disappointed."

Saralena's eyes widen. "Not me! I'd have been the happiest woman on earth! I still don't know what we did wrong."

"I'd have been happy, too," Sonia agrees, "because I still believed the ERA would raise women's status."

Mattie snorts. "Silly you!"

"Yeah, silly me!" Sonia laughs, then says seriously, "But toward the end of the ERA campaign I finally did see the futility of it all. I saw that men own the law; in fact, that they *are* the law: they make it, they interpret it, and they enforce it, and always so it benefits them. If the ERA had passed, they'd almost certainly have figured out how to make it work less for women than for themselves, as is their wont."

"Of course," Jade says. "That's what patriarchy means: Male privilege *über alles*."

Sonia turns back to Saralena. "So what did we do wrong? Well, the conventional answers are that we didn't do enough, or that we didn't do the right things, or that we weren't radical enough, or that we defeated our cause by being too radical."

"Don't forget the part about how we didn't keep the Lesbians hidden," Jade adds.

"Fat chance!" Mattie snorts, "since we were the majority of feminist activists, doing most of the heavy lifting and . . ."

Saralena finishes the sentence, "and caring most about women, in every way, all the time. Enough to put our reputations, our jobs, and even our lives on the line."

"Well," Mattie sighs, "being discounted isn't anything new for Lesbians."

"You talk about being a 'feminist' activist, Mattie," Elinor switches the subject, "but so do women with very different ways of looking at the world. To leaders of the national women's organizations, feminism meant getting women into the game of politics. They believed that if women were elected to office, they could change the way the game was played.

"But what we saw over and over again was that when they did get into the game, not only could they not change it but it could—and did—change them instead."

"And usually not in desirable ways," Sonia adds.

Mattie nods. "You're right, of course. And when women did get into the game and didn't change it, the women who'd helped get them elected felt betrayed. They hadn't realized that being in the game makes women even less effective than when they were just booing from the bleachers. They didn't understand that that's the definition of 'co-optation': neutralizing your enemies by giving them a stake in your system."

"Remember how when you tried to explain this to women, they'd totally discount you?" Mattie says. "How they'd say, 'Well, what else can we do? Politics is the only game in town'?"

Sonia sighs. "Unfortunately, they were right; it was the only game in town—actually the only game in patriarchy. I know that now. But I refused to believe it then, and their insisting made me frantic. I knew that politics as usual would just get us more politics as usual, that there had to be something else. In my naiveté I'd say things like, 'How about inventing our own game?'"

"Still sounds good to me!" Elinor says.

"To me, too, Elinor," Sonia confesses, "but I was so new to the Movement I didn't realize we already had invented our own game—or reinvented it for the umpteenth time." Seeing puzzled faces, she explains, "I'm talking about Sisterhood."

"Sisterhood," Elinor pretends to muse. "I do seem to remember hearing that word somewhere . . . a long, long time ago. Will someone please remind me what it means?"

"Sure," Jade offers. "How's this? Sisterhood is what transforms a woman's life when she finally understands that she has more in common with any woman than she has with any man."

"Wow, sister, that's the stuff of revolution!" Mattie exclaims, only partly in jest. "That could change the world!"

"It can," Jade agrees, "and I think it ultimately will."

"Once upon a time it did," Sonia adds. "Once it was the basis of a totally unified female world—I call it the SisterWitch Connection."

Elinor says, "Hey! I like the sound of that. What was it?"

"It was a bond—an unimaginably powerful bond—among and between females of every species," Sonia answers. "A universal Sisterhood so profound and so amazing that there's no language for it. Certainly there has never been anything even remotely like it on this planet anywhere since the onset of patriarchy.

"But before that it was such a part of our essence as females that men have never been able to destroy it totally. To this day, fragments of it float about in our memories. Sometimes I think that may be why we loved even our very imperfect Sisterhood back in the day—because the euphoria we felt in the community of the Women's Movement resembled the spiritual arousal we had experienced daily in that world."

"Sounds like you're talking about an archetype—the 'real' or 'original' Sisterhood," Elinor says, "and that you think the best of what we've experienced in our time is a sort of psychic echo of it."

Sonia grins and gives her a quick hug. "That's perfect, Elinor—a 'psychic echo!'"

"You can have it, if you want. But what were SisterWitches?"

"Well, I call them SisterWitches," Sonia replies, "because there's no ready-made word for them. I know SisterWitches doesn't convey what they were, but it's the best I can think of. These were women who were infinitely more than either the word 'sister' or 'witch' alone but in conjunction the meanings of these two words hint at certain rare qualities about them— 'sister' being our most egalitarian female relationship, and 'witch' connoting female power that transcends human limits.

"Of course, out of their fear of women's power, men have always called witches evil, and people in general still mistakenly think of them this way—partly because sham 'witches' sometimes act out that role in malign ways. But for me, the SisterWitch Connection conjures up an undeviatingly ethical, infinitely powerful, pre-male, pre-matriarchal, pre-goddess Sisterhood. A sisterhood that's still part of us."

"Yeah, but seriously," Mattie interrupts, uncomfortable with the visionary Sonia, "getting back to the real world. In my opinion, it wasn't any 'psychic echo' that formed the basis of whatever feelings of Sisterhood we had back in the day; it was Consciousness Raising. To me, this made CR the most brilliant and unifying—most feminist—aspect of the Women's Movement. It helped us understand that we weren't alone, and that, in fact, we shared with women everywhere in the world the experience of being oppressed by a misogynist system."

"But if the Sisterhood game was so smart," Saralena asks, "why didn't we keep playing it instead of resorting to politics as usual?"

"Well, for one thing, in a woman-hating world it's an almost impossible game even to conceive of, let alone to play," Sonia answers.

"And," Elinor says cynically, "our leaders didn't consider it politically expedient."

"Right on!" Mattie agrees. "That was pretty much the first priority. I was very active in the National Organization for Women, and I never heard any leader in that organization talk about how being a feminist could even change the way you ran an organization, let alone the world. They didn't offer any better model to women than men did."

"I was there, too," Jade says, "and it was misogyny as usual in our own organization, a sort of competition to see who could be the best junior man."

Mattie nods. "Sisterhood wasn't only *not* a common goal, it wasn't really a goal at all. Very few of the leaders—but to be fair, few of us—had any larger dream than to get a bigger piece of the pie."

Elinor laughs. "A piece of patriarchy's poisoned pie; good alliteration but a yucky goal."

"So what all of you seem to be saying is that we missed the boat," Saralena concludes. "Did it even float by?"

"Sure it did!" Mattie says. "And you're right—I do think we missed it. I agree with Sonia. We were so seduced by politics we didn't realize that the right boat, the one named 'Sisterhood,' was at the dock waiting for us and that that was where our real power lay: changing the way we felt about ourselves, not the way men felt about us; learning to love our female selves and all other women; treating all women as sisters—dropping men's hate-filled -isms about color, size, age, class, and nationality.

"I think changing our hearts could have changed the world, and if we'd taken that boat, well, we might have ended up with something really new!"

"Maybe, maybe not." Sonia says skeptically. "But I must say we gave it our best try. We talked a lot about how patriarchy's hatred of all things female was alive and well in us—'internalized oppression,' remember? I'll never forget how hard we each tried to find ways to locate it in ourselves so we could root it out. And how disillusioned we were when, try as we might, we couldn't seem to make headway against it."

Elinor sighs. "I remember all right. Unfortunately, we have lots of proof that internalized oppression is still alive and well. It turns up at every women's gathering in some fashion; we all saw it at the Hullaballoo in Santa Fe in 2007, for instance. It's still mostly there—the self-hatred and anger we project upon other women, the grief of our lives as females focused as blame and criticism upon other women."

"Well, it's because women are safe targets," Jade reminds them. "It's too dangerous to direct our anger at men where it really belongs. So, like the oppressed people we are, we rage at one another and defend our oppressors."

"Exactly," Sonia agrees. "And of course we're not conscious of our motives, or that in fighting one another we do exactly what men want us to do.

"But I can't lay any blame on the leaders of the women's organizations for not being more enlightened about the basis of real change. Back then, just like now, feminism—Sisterhood, if you will—wasn't generally understood to be a complete worldview in itself, an entirely new way of interpreting and experiencing everything, a whole new habit of mind.

"Instead, for most Movement leaders, as for most of us, feminism simply meant equal rights in the system as it existed. It meant 'issues'—abortion rights, equal pay, the ERA."

Saralena's head shoots up. "Whoa, wait a minute," she counters. "Don't knock those 'issues'! They were very important to a lot of us!"

"That's true," Jade says, "but I think what Sonia's saying is that they were not part of a basically different worldview; they were all futile attempts to fit women justly into the basically unjust systems of male privilege. There was no understanding that equal rights are an oxymoron in any hierarchy—the definition of hierarchy, after all, is that some are more equal than others. So, by definition, so long as men control the world they'll be more equal than women, and equal rights for the rest of us will be impossible."

Sonia adds, "To change this configuration—men on top and women on the bottom—is not an equal rights issue; it's really not an 'issue' at all. It demands a whole new non-hierarchical world, a profound understanding and rejection of patriarchy. Feminists of the sixties knew this, and that the first step was freeing themselves from men's domination."

"Otherwise, no SisterPower," Saralena summarizes.

"Right, Saralena," Sonia says. And you can tell how seriously they took freedom from the title they gave their new movement: The Women's Liberation Movement. Now there's a brave and portentous name for you!"

Mattie leans forward eagerly. "As I've just been saying, Consciousness Raising was basic to the liberation part. Even though it was about women's private realizations—or *because* it was about them—it was a deeply seditious act, with huge political potential. Anyway, generally speaking, many feminists of the sixties and early seventies knew that true liberation was first and foremost an inside job, personal and individual. They knew that these internal victories were the ones upon which any external victories depended, and that CR could help us win those victories."

Elinor nods, says, "I agree that the radicalizing effect of CR upon our personal relationships gave us the courage to unmask publically the system's terrorist tactics against women as a caste. So, like you, Mattie, I was dismayed that our leaders' obsession with political issues blinded them to the revolutionary meaning of 'the personal is political.'"

"Probably most impressive and influential to me as an emerging feminist," Mattie says, "was the model of courage feminists gave me. For the first time in my life I saw self-respecting women, women who refused to beg men for anything; strong, fearless women who didn't grovel. With our own eyes we saw women for whom prostrating themselves before men was not only no longer acceptable behavior but hardly even possible."

Elinor takes it up. "They encouraged and inspired us to be braver than we thought we could be; to love freedom so much we got up off our knees and testified against our captivity in every way we could think of!"

She looks around the table. "Okay, you can smile at our impassioned rhetoric. But every one of you knows how thrilling our new-found feminist courage felt, how ardently we believed in ourselves and the righteousness of our cause, how liberated we felt when for the first time in our lives we declared openly—and politically acted on—our love for women!"

Saralena leaps to her feet, raises her fist, and shouts, "Together we rose and *roared.*"

When the whistling and clapping subsides, Elinor , suddenly sober, says, "So obviously, we had to be stopped."

"Right on!" Mattie agrees. "And politicians relied on their allies in the women's organizations to stop us. So while paying lip-service to CR, for example, they actually blew it off as just so much touchy-feely fluff."

Sonia leans forward. "Not to excuse them, but you know, rebuilding the world according to a female pattern had never been part of their agenda. I'm not sure they believed such a pattern existed—actually, it was pretty vague even to those of us who *did* believe it. I don't think it ever entered their minds that the world could be significantly different than it was and that women were the only ones who could recreate it. I'm not even sure they'd have wanted a female-generated world."

"Let's not forget," Jade takes it up, "that from their beginnings, the purpose of the national women's organizations was political, not feminist in the sense we mean that word. Party politics was where their first allegiance lay. Right off the bat, they began serving as the handmaidens of the men's political parties—their Ladies' Auxiliaries, if you will."

Sonia laughed. "You got it! Like the Relief Society, the mormon sisterhood for the brotherhood. Wouldn't they have been horrified to learn that they were behaving just like the right-wing church women they found so misguided and pathetic!"

She pauses, says soberly, "But then, in a very real sense, so were all us ERA supporters. Like a steam-roller on a mission, the urgency of our political agenda overrode and obliterated most of our feminist philosophical considerations."

"So," Mattie moves determinedly on, "that co-optation—or perhaps more kindly—that original political purpose of the national women's organizations shifted the direction of the whole Movement. It focused our attention away from regaining a sense of our own centrality and power, right back to men and their political games. Just like old times, we found ourselves men's toadies and footpads, a movement with no philosophy of liberation whatsoever."

Elinor nods. "Well put, Mattie. Imagine how scary the word 'liberation' must have seemed back then. There our women leaders were in Washington, D. C., trying to look politically cool and savvy, like seasoned politicians, while we wild-eyed radicals kept hurling explosive words like 'liberation' around the country."

"How hysterical and overwrought of us!" Mattie exclaims. "How foolish to be taking our little 'women's issues' as seriously as men had always taken their big important ones—like what country to invade next!"

Elinor shakes her head with mock solemnity. "Silly us," she tsks.

"Worse yet," Mattie adds, "the word 'liberation' carried the clear implication that men had enslaved us. Think how *that* must have charmed the politicians our leaders were trying to influence!"

Elinor nods. "So, to conclude the sorry tale, that pesky word disappeared and suddenly there we were, no longer the Women's Liberation Movement but just another docile ladies auxiliary, doing mountains of work for men's political parties and getting mountains of nothing in return."

"All true, of course," Mattie muses. "But I often think that even if we'd remained the Women's Liberation Movement, even if we'd been able to make some headway with our internalized oppression and keep Sisterhood central, we couldn't have changed things much. Men still ruled, patriarchy was still the behemoth of this planet, maybe of the universe. Men could have—and would have—destroyed us all in a second if they'd thought we posed a serious danger to them."

"But we'll never know, will we," Elinor says, "because we were never a threat to men's control and they knew it."

"I disagree," Sonia argues. "I think we were a serious threat, as evidenced by their fierce backlash that finally did destroy us as a movement. In our tremendous passion for freedom, our potential for overthrowing men's system of female slavery was real and dangerous. And believe me, it scared them. That's why they had to neutralize us.

"Co-opting our organizations was just one part of that plan, as was derailing the ERA. Quietly—the invisibility of it causing it to be all the more devastating—men in control marshaled all the engines of male privilege to quash our uprising—and our spirits: the media, legislatures, courts, churches, universities, corporations. The propaganda and policy machines of all the institutions of patriarchy were drafted into emergency service to manipulate the opinions and policies of the world, to covertly fan the flames of woman-hatred and fear of female power, to get the slaves back in line and preserve male mastery. Susan Faludi's book, *Backlash, The Undeclared War Against American Women* (Doubleday: NY, 1991), gives us a blow-by-blow description of that battle.

"Each of us here, along with feminists everywhere, struggled against this backlash, most of us unconscious of its origins. But finally, not really understanding what was happening or how, we were swept apart in the resulting feminist diaspora, our hopes destroyed, our community in disarray."

She pauses, then finishes, "It's still in disarray, as you know, all of us aware that we will never be able to reconstruct that time, or its wonderful ambience. But I don't think it was all wasted . . ."

"No, Sonia!" Elinor interrupts, banging her fist on the table; everyone jumps, startled. "Don't try to mitigate it! It was evil what they did; somebody just needs to come out and say it! We were so trusting, so easy to manipulate, so thoroughly brainwashed to believe in the superiority of all things male and in the inevitability of their world!"

She rages on. "It was so easy—it's still so easy—to lead women down the primrose path. None of us—not Lesbians, not feminists, none of us—could take our eyes off the guys. Stockholmed to the hilt, none of us could dream a dream independent of them. And the unbearable irony is that they co-opted the beautiful energy of our vision of women's freedom and used it to keep us chained to the system!"

She flings herself back in her chair, her eyes shiny with furious tears. "I really hate them!"

For a few seconds she struggles for composure, then, her voice still shaking with emotion, says, "So the question is, do I honestly think there will ever be a time when we will be free? I guess I have to answer no; no, I don't."

"Elinor," Sonia says, taking her hand, "we will be free, and perhaps soon. But it won't happen the way we thought it would, or in any way we could have imagined back then. I look around and see that now, without any organized help from us, mensworld is careening to its destruction. I believe there's nothing we can do to speed it up or to slow it down. Its deadly drama on the stage of the universe is in Act 5, Scene 5, the final curtain about to come down with no encores."

Elinor rolls her eyes, says cynically, "Oh yeah, right."

"Yeah, right," Sonia says calmly.

Jade turns to Elinor. "I feel it in my bones, Elinor, and my whole intuitive self confirms it. But it's powerfully reinforced by something my Native American friend, Jesse Raven Tree, taught me nearly 30 years ago."

She looks around the table, sees the blank faces of her friends. "I've told you about Jesse, haven't I? No? Well, let's get up for a few minutes, stretch, get a drink, get comfortable. And then, if you like, I'll tell you a story."

Chapter 2

Jade's Story

Jesse Raven Tree and I met one day in the summer of 1980 shortly after I moved to the Southwest. I was picking sage and dreaming in the warm sun when a rustling in the brush caused me to glance up. There just a few feet away stood a wizened old woman holding her own sage-harvesting sack and regarding me steadily with sharp black eyes. As I straightened up, she walked over and asked for a ride back to her home.

She climbed into my car and into my life that afternoon, initiating a brief but extraordinarily intense and life-changing friendship.

As if she hadn't much time and wanted to get past the preliminaries quickly, she shut the car door and began at once to summarize her life for me.

She was 101 or 102 years old, she thought, born and raised to young teen-age in an ancient Native American matriarchal tradition before it began to be systematically destroyed by the missionaries. When they arrived, they took her from her tribe to live with an Anglo family; it was this family who recognized how brilliant she was and sent her to one of the most prestigious universities in the world.

There she earned a doctorate in genetics and became an authority on mutations, among the first scientists to find and study the y chromosome. As our friendship developed, I came to know the intrepid scientist she was as well as the visionary feminist.

That first day in the car, she told me matter-of-factly that she had no daughters or other female relatives who were interested in the old beliefs and traditions she had learned as a girl. This was the reason she had been waiting for me, she said, to pass on to me this crucial information and keep it from being lost.

Having said this, from her overburdened heart she began at once to pour forth a flood of memories, stories, and beliefs that the women of her clan had preserved down through the ages. A year-long flood that stopped only when her heart stopped.

Though she has been in the spirit realm now for many years, I feel as if she is right here beside me much of the time, particularly as I sleep. She had things she wanted me to know and do, and she is too passionate, even in death, to stay demurely on the sidelines when women are in peril, as she knew we were even before she died.

Her impatience with me when I couldn't make sense of things, when I didn't respond appropriately, when I couldn't answer a question; her quick anger at my outbreaks of patriarchal indoctrination and conditioning—this fierceness at first kept me wary of her. But I came to realize that it betrayed only her passion and her very great haste to make me understand. Fervently pro-woman and dauntingly intelligent, she ran a tough school in which I often felt mystified, overwhelmed, and not-quite-bright.

I had to remind myself sometimes that I was almost 70 years younger than she, from an alien world, an alien language and culture, an alien time. So it was hardly surprising that her training made me stretch—emotionally and intellectually— more than was always comfortable.

But I'm glad she persisted. Now I live with memories of the magical female world she laid shimmering before me then, as well as with an intuitive understanding of what she considered so imperative for me to know that she delayed her death for a year to entrust it to me.

Surprisingly, it was all about women, never about Native American customs per se, customs she believed had become mere male attempts to emulate female power.

She was seriously alarmed that the women of her tribe had now forgotten the one story more important to remember than any other in their tradition. Again and again she told me this story, always prefacing it with the comment that if I remembered nothing else of what she said, I must remember this. It was the most ancient belief of her tribe, the very opening words of their sacred oral history:

Once all things were female.

Everything had been female forever, she taught me, with no beginning and no end. This totally female world was loving and peaceful, without illness or pain or suffering of any kind, every living thing experiencing only joy.

Then, following a gigantic explosion in the universe, maleness began to appear among most species—a consequence that soon proved catastrophic.

But women understood and passed down through countless generations of women the information that this deadly species would eventually die out, and ultimately all would be female and life-loving again.

Jesse always ended this story by looking into my eyes and saying emphatically, 'I believe that time is at hand.'

What surprised me was not her story, though I knew how crazy it should have sounded. What surprised me was that I believed it at once, finding it as deeply familiar as if I'd always known it. To hear it again, to *remember* it—I can't express my relief.

Years later, when I told Sonia this story one afternoon as we sat before the wood fire in my little adobe house, she leapt to her feet in excitement. She had recently heard the same story from women who knew Australian Aboriginal beliefs. These clans, as a form of verification of their beliefs, claim to be the oldest extant people on earth, their oral history reaching farther back into the mists of antiquity than that of any others—and always in the keeping of women, as with Jesse's tribe.

Sonia and I sat together that afternoon in a warm haze of hope, marveling that two ancient peoples on opposite sides of the globe had preserved the memory of this world as having been inhabited solely by female beings for eons before the advent of males. We both got goose bumps talking about the Aboriginal women's echo of Jesse's prophecy that someday all would be female again, and that *that time was at hand.*

ᘯ ᘯ ᘯ

After Jade stops talking, the group sits thinking quietly for a moment. Then Elinor turns to her.

"Did Jesse ever elaborate upon this; you know, give details?" she asks.

Jade nods. "Oh, yes. She talked about it often. Maleness had been the subject of most of her genetic research, and she was among the first of many geneticists to hold that it was a mutation. This must have been in the 1940's and 1950's, so it's certainly not a new idea, having been around for at least 60 years. Most of us have run across it somewhere though we probably didn't take it literally.

But she was very literal about it, having shown through her research that men demonstrate a mutation's classic characteristics: inability to adapt to the environment, violence, and destructiveness, and—in geological terms, at least—a short existence as a species."

"Not short enough for me," Elinor mutters.

Jade continues. "Jesse told me that because mutations in a large species can't adapt to their environment, they cause enormous upheaval and disorder. Also, being the exact opposite of the parent species—in this case, females—they are inherently as destructive as females are creative, destroying themselves, one another, and the environment necessary for their survival. Eventually they run out of genetic material and life energy, and become extinct."

At this, Mattie looks up and says, "Actually, standing in line at the checkout in Natural Grocers a couple of weeks ago, I read something very like this. I picked up a magazine called *Mental Floss* (Mar.-Apr. 2008) because the headline intrigued me: "The Future of Sex: The Death of the Y Chromosome." The article itself was a disappointment, but at least it mentioned Bryan Sykes and his book, *Adam's Curse: A Future Without Men*. I didn't read the book, but apparently he argues that the y chromosome is rapidly becoming extinct."

She looks around at the surprised and interested faces of her friends, and shrugs her shoulders apologetically. "I told you I didn't read the book." She turns to Jade for help.

"I haven't been reading the research either," Jade confesses, "though I know there's lots of it out there now available on the internet. Friends are sending us sites to check all the time. But because I believe Jesse and the women of her tribe, and choose to believe the Aboriginal women, I don't need the research of male experts to convince me. Without having heard a syllable from them, I've believed in men's extinction for 30 years.

"When Jesse talked to me about this long ago, I asked her for the quick-and-easy explanation, without all the scientific language. She gave me this analogy, after reminding me that, like all analogies, it had its limitations. In my own words, then, as I remember it:

"Let's say we have two horseshoe-shaped magnets. One of these represents femaleness because it has two live poles—that is, two large X chromosomes. Since these continually recharge each other, this magnet never loses its energy.

"Maleness is represented by a horseshoe-shaped magnet which has only one live pole—its sole X chromosome. The other pole, representing the small y chromosome, has no energy at all. The live pole can hold a charge but it can't create or renew it because the other pole is not only unable to reenergize it but actually takes energy from it. So the magnet with only one live pole has to be recharged frequently by the double-energy-creating magnet.

"For awhile, these infusions of energy do the job—the charge holds. But over time, the one-live-poled magnet, unable to maintain its own charge, becomes less and less able to hold the charge from the two-live-poled magnet, and finally loses this capacity altogether. At this point, the mutation comes to the end of its genetically predetermined lifespan."

"And not a moment too soon!" Elinor says.

"Oh Elinor, don't be so bitter," Saralena scolds her gently. "It just hurts you. For your own sake, try to forgive them."

"Hey," Mattie interrupts, "let's not get into forgiveness here. If we do, I'm afraid we won't leave this house still friends."

"Forgiveness is an act of great power," Saralena persists. "It would help you to forgive men, too, Mattie."

Mattie shakes her head. "Never!"

Sonia leans across and asks, "What's forgiveness got to do with it, Saralena? It's really irrelevant, like forgiving mosquitoes for living off our blood. They don't do it on purpose. It's just part of what it means to be a mosquito. Understanding that men are genetically parasites and destroyers makes forgiveness as irrelevant for them as it is for mosquitoes. It's just part of what it means to be male."

"I think that's a bad analogy!" Saralena protests.

"I'm sure you realize, Sonia, and you, too, Jade," Mattie interjects, "that even suggesting that biology is destiny opens you to accusations of prejudice and ignorance. The 'biology is destiny' doctrine is so bigoted and so passé it's not even inflammatory anymore. Women aren't going to listen to what they perceive as rampant political incorrectness."

Jade raises her eyebrows. "So? Who's trying to convince them? I think Jesse was right: whether it's politically correct or not, for both men and women biology *is* destiny."

"And try to remember when men last told the truth," Elinor whispers to Mattie.

Mattie doesn't look happy. "I know, I know," she says impatiently. "But a world without men is completely unrealistic and for most women totally undesirable. Damned few women would choose to live in a male-free world!"

"Then they won't have to; they can follow men out of women's universe, out of existence, if they wish," Sonia says. "And it's not a call to action, either, Mattie. It's not a mandate for women to get out there and kill men—though some may think that's a pretty fine idea. Right, Elinor?

"Anyway, if Jesse and others are right, women can neither slow this process down nor accelerate it. It has its own agenda and will carry it through regardless of what we do or believe. I agree that most women will go right on supplying men with life energy right up to the instant men can't receive it any longer. And frankly, Elinor, that instant can't arrive too soon for me, either."

She continues: "I not only hope it happens soon; I already *see* it happening. Right before our eyes the male social-political-economic system is falling apart at lightning speed. It's in chaos worldwide. And Sykes is not the only geneticist proclaiming the demise of maleness.

"Add to this the information that impotence is affecting large and increasing numbers of men, among them many young ones; and that fertility clinics report that male sterility is now the major issue in their field, some estimating that at least 50 percent of males under 40 are sterile; and that studies show males rapidly losing genes from their chromosomes; and that out of the skyrocketing number of babies being spontaneously aborted or stillborn, or born with serious defects, a hugely disproportionate number are male.

"Just as Jesse predicted, they're losing genetic material and the capacity to hold their parasitically-obtained life energy."

She pauses, adds, "but if their genetic past-due date doesn't arrive fast enough, there are always their nuclear playthings waiting in the wings to finish the job. And, of course, the incalculable damage they've done to their environment.

"So it seems to me it's not a question of 'if' they're self-destructing, or maybe even 'when'—I mean, it's really no longer even about them. If it's out of women's hands, it's also out of men's. Men are on their way out no matter what anyone likes or doesn't like, what they or anyone else does or doesn't do.

"What matters now is that females survive the cataclysm men cause as they take their leave. What matters is that we keep our promise to the planet and to one another to be, if possible, physically present with as much female energy as we can muster, as we and our sisters—the planet and all female beings universe-wide—struggle to survive and re-emerge in our true, and truly immense, beauty and power.

"But you know something? Even if it's not necessary for as many women as possible to survive in the flesh—though I'm pretty sure it is—and even if I didn't have promises to keep, I want passionately to be here for the whole thing: the return of the female universe, the reassembling and reuniting of all female beings, the return of absolute health and safety, joy and peace. And love—finally the real thing!

"I want to experience it all flowing—no, *surging*—back again, every iota, every second of it. I want to *taste* it, *hear* it, *feel* it, *smell* it, *SEE* it. I've waited for this for—what? 25,000 years? Longer? Anyone who thinks I'd miss it now is out of her mind!"

"But, Sonia," Elinor says with mock earnestness, "weren't you the one who advised us to go out of our minds?"

Sonia sticks her tongue out at her.

As if she has been listening only to her own thoughts during this, Saralena now says pensively, "I wanted equal rights so much, you know. It just seemed fair. But that about sums up what I knew about feminism. I wish I'd paid more attention to the other stuff you were all talking about back then, because now I'm full of questions."

"Such as?" Elinor asks.

"Well, you all talk about patriarchy, but what is it exactly? How did men take over the world? And . . ."

She stops, flustered. Everyone waits. Then in a small sad voice she finishes: ". . . why do they hate us so much?"

Sonia jumps up from the table, goes into the living room, and reappears with a sheaf of papers. Laying it on the table in front of Saralena, she explains, "This is the finished draft of the book I've been writing—or at least I thought it was finished. But as you were talking, I realized that nowhere in it have I actually defined patriarchy, and that there will be others like you who will need to know what I mean by that term in order to understand this book."

She smiles at Saralena, "So I'm going to remedy that omission tonight in some new pages; I'll put them on top of the manuscript so that my definition of patriarchy will be the first thing you read.

"You know, when I began this book, I hoped to be able to write it completely about women without once referring to men. But of course this is impossible; our history as far back as time goes has been so totally entwined with theirs that we are largely now what *we* are because they are what *they* are.

"So the book deals—mostly peripherally but sometimes centrally—with *your* questions about men, Saralena, as I try to answer *my* questions about women: What is femaleness? Who are women? What were we like originally? Where did we come from? What is our destiny?"

Chapter 3

Patriarchy and Maleness

I wish, Saralena, that in the book you're about to read I could have found some way to avoid using the word "patriarchy." But as much as all of us would like to forget it, and someday will, this term is still the only accurate word we have for the world we live in: a world devised by men, owned by men, and run by men. Because of this, it has always offended some women and threatened others and seems to have gone almost totally out of fashion since the mid-1980's.

Thinking back about it now, though, I realize that it was commonly used only in radical feminist parlance even then, so it was never really what you'd call fashionable. Though no one would ever have expected to hear it from the mouth of the national president of NOW, out of fear of men even radical feminists had trouble saying it. It was tantamount to waving a red flag announcing, "I hate men!" And then waiting, terrified, to be forced off a lonely road some night.

So women who fear the word "patriarchy" are right: it *is* dangerous; male supremacy is precisely and openly what it denotes: the rule—the "archy"—of the fathers. Men, intent on keeping their machinations invisible to us, very much dislike having the hierarchy—i.e., the sadomasochism—that is the foundation of their every system of thought and action exposed in this way.

But what about matriarchy, you say; that's —archy and sadomasochism, too, isn't it?

Yes, but different in many ways. Matriarchy, for instance, had to have post-dated the advent of men. Before maleness, hierarchy was utterly unknown to females. Having no need for it, we had no concept of governance or control—not even self-control, since in us were no negative impulses, no hurtful desires, no destructive possibilities.

After maleness arrived in the universe, however, bearing hierarchy in its genetic makeup, matriarchies began to appear as women's reaction to men, our attempts to curtail and miti-gate male rapaciousness and bring it under some semblance of control.

But in sadomasochism (i.e., the wielding of control), fe-males, for whom hierarchy is unnatural, could never compete with men. Being *in essence* an-archic, non-violent beings, we were unable to hold out against newcomers who were not only willing but eager to torture and kill to gain control, eager to destroy whatever stood in their way.

In males sadomasochism is innate. Central to everything they think and do, it overrides not only all other motives and considerations, but all sense. The irrational ideation and be-havior that springs from this genetic handicap baffles women; think how often we ask each other in bewilderment, "What can they be *thinking?*"

Sadomasochism's fleeting zing is the male substitute for the lasting ecstasy of being that we knew as females before the advent of maleness. This zing is more than an overpowering addiction; for men, it is necessary for life.

However, since patriarchy *is* sadomasochism *is* hierarchy and we are all trapped in patriarchal ontology, none of us can escape sadomasochistic thought and behavior; it is the foun-dation and substance of our current world mind, the basis of everyone's every transaction and relationship in men's world, no matter who they are.

Why, then, don't I view sadomasochism simply as a human trait, innate also in females? Because unlike men, women *as a species* do not, for instance, exhibit the need to wage wars, to murder or enslave or starve people, to torture and maim them, or to take control of their countries and exploit their resources. The cruelty and violence that provide the temporary thrill of sadomasochism that men mistakenly call power is absent from us *as a species*. They are, in fact, the opposite of women's inclinations and behavior in the world.

(Just one more piece of evidence, Saralena, that women are not human at all. But more of this later.)

Sadomasochism may not be an innate characteristic of femaleness, but no one could argue that women are free of it. Now, after millennia of painful exposure to patriarchal thought and behavior, universally we are contaminated by it—some of us more, some less. And until maleness no longer exists in the world—and hence no longer exists in *us*—we can only moderate it in our behavior, never entirely rid ourselves of it no matter how hard we try. Nevertheless, though currently intractable, it is for us a superficial condition, not part of our essence.

Tonight at the table you asked, "Where did patriarchy come from?"

Let me go back a little.

A paradigm such as patriarchy is a worldview, a closed system of values, ideas, behaviors, needs, possibilities, beliefs, and desires. It is presumed to explain everything and to be the one and only possible interpretation of all phenomena.

Males came into this universe bearing their entire paradigm within themselves. Inherent in maleness, patriarchy is its genetic essence-become-ontology; it is the philosophy that corresponds to male innerness, fitting, describing, explaining, and justifying it.

What this means is that people did not simply wake up one morning, look out their windows, and exclaim to one another: "Oh, look! During the night patriarchy fell all over everything—just like snow!" It means that patriarchy did not come out of nowhere and that we are not all, male and female, equally accountable for it or similarly vulnerable to its abuses.

As a way of viewing and interpreting everything, of structuring all thought and action, as a complete ontology, patriarchy came and continues to come directly out of the primal impulses, the deepest longings and desires—the *essence*—of male beings. It is what they *are*, their natural and ineluctable mode of existence. As a worldview, or paradigm, it is spawned from what is necessary for them to live, what they value, what they believe is real, true, and possible—and actually all that *is* possible for them.

Projected from their internal world out upon the external world as behaviors and systems, patriarchy is a revelation to us of men's most hidden inner selves.

This is why we do not have to look any farther than at the world they have made to understand clearly what men most profoundly and essentially are. The day we stop believing what they say and look clear-eyed at their behavior and its consequences instead, refusing to make any more excuses for them—that's the day we will be able to see and know them. When we do, we will begin to understand ourselves and how profoundly "not-them" we are.

In a nutshell, another name for patriarchy—the entire global regime under whose tyranny we bow—is maleness. Since patriarchy is men's essence, every detail of it elucidates—and warns us about—their species.

꙰ ꙰ ꙰

A Few of the Fallacies Deliberately and Cunningly Propagated by the Toxic-Age Fathers to Obscure the Fact—and Implications—of Patriarchy

The Toxic-Age Movement—that profoundly male-serving ideology that cunningly calls itself "New Age"—propounds, no, *preaches* as the same old religion it is (with "the universe" filling in for "god," only more so), that men and women, except for their socialization, are essentially the same. So why blame all the bad stuff on men? If we're all alike, all one, we're all in this together—right?

Wrong. But that's what men would like us to believe. If they can succeed in obscuring and even erasing the significance of gender differences—particularly the notion that maleness is totally *other* than femaleness—the awareness of patriarchy's existence goes deeply into hiding. This subterfuge—that men have the same feelings and values as women—gives men easy and unlimited access to the female energy that is, quite literally, life to them.

To support the fable of essential male and female sameness, Toxic-Age men insist that gender is mutable, changeable from one life to the next: women have been men in other lives and may be men again in the future (so how can women be critical of them?); and men have lived lives as women (so women can trust them).

As part of this indoctrination, Toxic-Age women have also been manipulated into accepting men's teaching that gender occurs along a continuum from "masculine" to "feminine," that these are both learned modes of being, and that neither of them is exclusive, inherent, or unchangeable.

In reality, however, the constructs of "masculinity" and "femininity" are shrewdly designed to obscure the profound and immutable differences between males and females. Meant to deflect our attention from the mountains of evidence that would prove these differences, the feminine/masculine strategy (as opposed to the male/female truth) has been among the fathers' most successful in winning women's trust.

Toxic-Age writing about women almost exclusively uses words and behaviors that describe the uncritical malleability of "feminine" rather than the strength and skepticism of "female." For obvious reasons, men much prefer "feminine"; femininity renders women controllable. (It is also attainable by men, whereas the strength, independence, and power of female are forever beyond their grasp. Men can be feminine but they cannot be female. Later, I will explain why they envy femaleness.)

Despite the centrality to patriarchy of the body/spirit dualism that provides the basis for their tenet of gender mutability, none of us is divisible in this way. Body and spirit (and mind and emotion and all the other supposed pieces of the shattered patriarchal psyche) are truly inseparable, truly one, our genes specifying spiritual as well as physical characteristics.

Ontologically, therefore, femaleness requires two spiritual/physical X chromosomes. Since women's spirits are genetically female and we are always the same spirit, our bodies also are always female. If we had not always been the same spirit, we would not have remained to this day both physically and spiritually affected by former lives.

Thus unchangeable and non-interchangeable from one life to another, our spirits fit and correspond to our bodies—*are* our bodies.

As Jesse Raven Tree taught, maleness, as a mutation of femaleness, is the *inversion* of femaleness, the reverse: men are women's antitheses, their complete opposites. None of us, women or men, turn our essential spirit/body selves inside out from one life to the next. We remain who we are, like it or not.

Males, therefore, constitutionally unable to meet the two-X-physical/spiritual-chromosome requirement, are forever prevented from being female—no matter how cleverly they imitate us, no matter how many operations they have, or hormones they take, or lives they live. The fact and implications of this are so intolerable to the patriarchal mind that men have generated much nonsense to veil, discount, and deny them.

True, there have always been some men and women who maintain that they are on this planet in the wrong bodies (and nowadays physically attempt to rectify this error), lending credence to Toxic-Age arguments that gender is not a given.

But whatever this confusion is about, the fact that it is widespread and increasing is hardly surprising. From its inception, patriarchy has been a brawling hodgepodge of cravings and obsessions, bringing ungovernable disorder to every square foot of the universe. But now in its end stage it is more tumultuous than ever before, and since it is universal—the paradigm of every planet as well as of the realms of the dead—all is chaos everywhere.

And not chaos in the positive, creative sense of the word but in the sense of messy meaninglessness. Maleness has made an unspeakable mess in the universe and now, as fate hauls it off the stage kicking and screaming, is barely able to keep itself together as a paradigm from one day to the next. Since this collapsing sadomasochistic structure is based upon gender, gender is bound to be the most controversial and misunderstood of all possible facts, as well as the most common cause for mix-ups.

And that's all they are—mix-ups, evidences of the entropy that is maleness.

Some Toxic-Age women believe the male-serving doctrine that we are reborn as different genders and species in order to learn important lessons. But, if this is true, the educational program of the "universe" is definitely not succeeding for males; men have never demonstrated that they have learned anything from it.

If men had indeed participated in this trans-migrational program and in other lives have been women (or any other animal, fish, bird, or insect of either gender), reason dictates that now, after thousands of years of such "schooling," they should be evincing more mercy, more peacefulness, more empathy and kindness, more respect for other living things than they did at the beginning of the experiment. If being women in other lives, for example, made any difference, we should be able to predict with some surety that men will now display—systematically, as individuals as well as a class—at least *some* female characteristics and values. And many fewer of them would be rapists.

But one look at their behavior in the world tells us that this is not the case, that in fact the opposite is true; a fact that casts serious doubt on the efficacy—not to mention the existence—of the "universe's" university.

Others explain that women sometimes come back as males (and vice versa for men) because we all need to have every possible experience. Why? Men's "every possible experience" seems to have caused immeasurable hurt and misery for themselves and others. No personal goals could possibly have been worth such anguish. Juvenile and narcissistic, this is merely Toxic-Age justification for the harm men do in their private and public lives. It denies the existence of evil, justifies terrorism, pleads innocence for blatant venality, and excuses ugly behavior with the old dodge that "everyone is doing it"—even women (the good guys) in their past lives as men. Insisting that they have to experience everything, men make the acting out of their vilest fantasies part of some higher, nobler scheme, one that is ultimately necessary for their full "development."

Development into what, and at whose expense?

We are a global community. Few women would agree that this community would benefit from their deciding to have "all possible experiences" in their next lives as males and coming back as rapists, serial murderers, and destroyers of their own species and planet. The women I know are not clamoring for the opportunity to "develop" themselves into such monsters.

Many Toxic-Agers deplore the dichotomous either/or categorizations of male/female, believing that "us/them" dichotomies not only are inaccurate but also cause contention and bigotry.

Dichotomous thinking in this case, however, is not just the result of ignorance or even of the innate duality of the patriarchal mind (the sadomasochistic mind that must always make comparisons —higher, lower; better, worse; kinder, crueler). "Either male *or* female" was the first true dichotomy to come into being, reflecting and accurately describing the ancient and unbreachable duality that was obvious to both females and males the first moment they tried to engage with each other—and smashed fatefully into the wall of their antithesis.

In the midst of burying and falsifying the truth of femaleness and maleness, patriarchy was born, men's lies about gender becoming its very foundation, structure, and substance. Suffusing every atom of patriarchy, gender bigotry—no, bigotry is too puny a word. Let me start again: Suffusing every atom of patriarchy, as men's lies do, fear and envy and hatred of all things female could stand alone as patriarchy's definition.

After all these millennia, however, the male world is disintegrating and dying right before our eyes.

You say it can't die? Oh yes, it can and it will, despite men's lie that it is ineluctable, the one and only possible world.

But what is the meaning of these thousands of years of maleness and patriarchy? What has it all been about? What purpose did it serve? What lessons was it meant to teach us? Did we learn them? In what ways was it part of the grand scheme of things?

Despite the insistence of religionists, including Toxic-Age adherents (and Alexander Pope), that whatever is, is right, was meant to be, and has a purpose, such illusions cannot be borne out in reality. Certainly, very little on this planet today is right, or has a purpose—other than satisfying men's calamitously burgeoning need for sadomasochistic "fixes."

Since there is neither a behind-the-scenes puppeteer nor a master—or mistress—plan, and no "grand scheme," nothing is "meant" to happen, either to individuals or worlds. Inescapable in the phrase "meant to be" is an agent who "means" it and guides matters to that end—god or the universe, some over-seer and organizer, some force that is alive and very much in control, the source of the "grand scheme."

But there is no such director, either beneficent or malefi-cent, not even nature. Nature is not a mother, not a role, not a caretaker. Since she is anarchic and controls nothing—makes no plans or rules or demands—she has nothing to enforce, no punishment to exact. Being female, nature simply *is*.

The truth is that nobody and nothing is cosmically "in charge" nor ever was. The universe—all universes—are anar-chic. To men, anarchy means mayhem only because they know the violence and mayhem inherent in themselves, and that it must be controlled if life is to continue. Anarchy is female, and femaleness—true and total power—needs no control. Free of time and sadomasochism, the anarchic female society works perfectly eon after eon.

Despite the current popular belief that there are no acci-dents and no coincidences, in fact accidents *do* happen, coin-cidences *do* occur in time-driven patriarchy—everywhere, all the time, with no particular purpose, conveying no particular message, playing no role in some overall preconceived design.

In the case of maleness, there was an accident in the universe—an immense accident—and from it, briefly, came maleness. Not because it was "meant to be," not because it had some goal to achieve, not to punish us, not to teach us lessons, not as some overseer's experiment, not to improve or destroy anything. Not for any purpose whatsoever.

Patriarchy was an accident, Saralena. It just happened. And it is becoming extinct for no other reason than because that's what mutations do. When it disappears, the female world will re-emerge, not because it was "meant to be" by anything or anyone, or because it has a role to play in some cosmic scheme of things, but simply because it never really left, has been here in female beings all along and, without the constraints of maleness, will open and unfold.

And unfold.

And unfold.

❧ ❧ ❧

PART II

The SisterWitch Way

Chapter 4

Timelessness: The SisterWitch Ambience

Once everything was female, had always been female—for countless eons, forever—never created, always existing, without beginning or end. Timeless.

Imagine!

Do you think we *can* imagine a timeless world?

Before the advent of maleness, what we know as time did not exist. No continuum stretched like a river from the beginning (since we had no beginning) through past, present, and future, on out to end (since we will have no end). Instead, like a dazzling double helix of creativity, everything that constituted being—energy, matter, intelligence, emotion, spirit, and power—was present at once. This made for a vast consciousness, one that was complex, multi-dimensional, and universal. A reality of unlimited possibility.

When we talk about timelessness as the ambience of women's world, the question that most often arises is, "If there is no linear time, how can the rising and setting of the sun, the seasons, birth and death, the growing of things—how can these be explained?"

The only honest response is to admit that since time is the foundation of the male paradigm we call patriarchy, it is so profoundly embedded in our psyches, so profoundly part of our universal mind and how we live in the world as women now, that we, like men, are essentially unable to think outside it. When we look at the sun rising and setting we can understand and experience it only in linear time. The next step is inevitable—we perceive the sunrise as a demonstration, as *proof*, of time and linearity: *first* the brightening of the horizon, *then* the fiery cusp rising above it, *now* the blazing globe flying free.

So our universal inability now to understand timelessness proves only how very conditioned we are to perceive every-thing as linear, as cause and effect, while proving nothing about the reality of sunset or sunrise, about seasons, or about birth and death. Even Einstein, when asked how his theory of relativity affected his everyday life, admitted that it made no difference at all, that though he could see the timeless world through the microscope, he could understand it only in the abstract. (This is from a reporter's interview with Einstein that I read at least fifty years ago and never forgot.)

Despite his great intelligence, however, even if he had been born into that timeless world as the first males were, he still could not have lived in it. Since maleness *is* time, men cannot escape the inevitability of it, and out of themselves impose it upon everything.

Twenty years ago, I wrote in *Wildfire: Igniting the She/Volution* (p. 219) that time is not a river but an ocean. It is not going anywhere. There is no past ocean, no present ocean, no future ocean. All the ocean that exists is right here, right now. Since I now understand that time and linearity are synony-mous, a less confusing word than "time" to describe that ocean might be "life" or "being"; instead of the ocean of time, then, the ocean of life, the ocean of being.

So in the timeless female universe, the fish in the ocean are born, grow old, and die (if indeed they do any of these things—and I believe they do not) because it is their nature. The flower we watch relax its fist and stretch its delicate fingers out into the morning coolness is not proof of time passing; it is only proof that the nature of that flower is to open into the sunshine. That is what that flower *is*, what its life looks like.

40

Not until maleness is gone, not until "doing" is gone (because doing requires us to be in linear time) and "being" is once again our mode, will females again be able to understand and live in a timeless, non-linear world. Only then will we escape means-to-ends, cause-and-effect, stimulus-response thought and behavior.

Though I have no intentional access to that world, on a few unforgettable occasions in my life I have serendipitously found myself in it again for a few moments. From this I know it is always just microseconds away from my full awareness. Memories of it also surface in dreams, or flit across my waking consciousness at odd moments—the aura of it, the vividness of sensory experience, the feelings unlike any I recognize from my life in mensworld.

The last time I suddenly found myself outside time for a few precious seconds was when the dogs and I were climbing near our home in New Mexico's Manzano Mountains. An ordinary New Mexico day, deep blue and bright gold. Climbing happily toward a meadow high above, I was stopped in my tracks by a sudden shift in my every sensory perception. The dogs stopped, too, and like me, stood absolutely still in an ocean of deepest silence.

The quality of this silence reminded me that, except for a few extraordinary moments like this, my life in patriarchy had always been accompanied by a sound—rather, a steady subliminal vibration—like the rushing of a great subterranean river. That day I recognized that the clamorous background against which we live our lives in patriarchy is time, and that *timelessness* was the stillness in which I then stood.

Not only is the river time a noise pollutant, it is also a psychic bully. Rushing relentlessly pell-mell through our lives, it intrudes, interrupts, nags, bosses us around. Sometimes, however, as prison guard or terrorist, it controls and frightens us. Part and parcel of maleness, time helps men control the world.

Timelessness is psychic and sensory stillness, non-polluting, clear, and clean. Timelessness is freedom and peace.

Though its utter silence first announces it, in my every experience of it timelessness also has had an amazing visceral effect. The instant I step unexpectedly into it, the surrounding world and I become huge, all-encompassing, opening out endlessly into a vast physical and emotional freedom and well-being—ecstasy, actually—that is unimaginable in men's puny little model of a world. What I am in the timelessness of the female world, what I have just described, is power.

I had serendipitously experienced a few precious moments of timelessness several times over the years preceding the one that fastened my dogs and me to the New Mexico mountainside. The one I remember most clearly took place one day in 1977, shortly before the night I awoke to myself as a woman in a mormon church meeting. Though I have written about it elsewhere, I want to remember it here as well.

I was driving down the country road near my home in Virginia on my way to the supermarket, enjoying the woods through the windows and the warm spring sun shining down through the trees, turning the new leaves almost a blinding fluorescent green.

But the sun was also heating up the car, so I began to roll down the window, and as I did, I glanced out again at the woods. Gone was the green I had just thought so amazing, and in its place blazed a green so quintessential, so lushly, lustily greener than any green could possibly be, that, looking at it in a sort of astonished recognition, I felt green through and through, as if my brain and my very thoughts were green, as if my blood were running green, as if I were a forest in full triumphant leaf. (I've since heard people who have taken various drugs talk about this same green, so I must stress that I was not under the influence of any intoxicating substance at the time of this event—and actually never have been. Mormonism was good for *something* at least!)

During that brief moment, I was in a timeless world, feeling vast, invulnerable, and ecstatically connected to and part of everything around me. For that brief moment, I was home.

"This is how the world really is!" I cried aloud. "This is how I really am!"

All the way to the store through the now dulled-out woods, I shook with excitement, marveling at what I had just experienced, and puzzling over what could have numbed my emotions so much that I had only now, at age forty, felt such joy for the first time. I didn't understand patriarchy then or its deadening basis in time. But being that forest for those few familiar seconds awakened in me an ancient homesickness, a longing for some other more enlivening, more inclusive life.

Now at this critical point in men's history and women's destiny, I am spurred by a great urgency to try to remember this world, my lost female homeland, to construct it, to re-mythologize it. Fortunately, Monique Wittig gives me two tools—memory and invention (from *Les Guerilles*, 1985; originally a prose paragraph):

There was a time
when you were not a slave.
Remember that.

You walked safely every
where, full of
*   laughter,*
you bathed barebellied.

You say you have lost all
recollection of this time.

You say there are no
words to describe it.
You say it does not exist.

But remember.
Make an effort
to remember.

Or, failing that,
invent.

Memory and invention—these are not the discrete, either-or tools they are often assumed to be. Instead they are inter-dependent, even inseparable, and very necessary to each other. Most people could not say with certainty where, in their own experience, one ends and the other begins; much of what we think is invention is in fact memory, and what we are sure is memory, actually invention. Without thought we focus them both at once upon a puzzle because each has access to different modes of consciousness; combined, they expand the like-lihood of our coming upon pieces of hidden knowledge and truth.

In this search for the truth of our female past and future, therefore, we can revitalize memory by inventing it, and create a more likely version of the story by remembering as much of it as we can.

Regardless of how we go about our individual searches and of how much absolute truth we uncover, I agree with Monique Wittig that we are obliged to try. So with her tools at hand, I begin remembering and inventing.

Chapter 5

The SisterWitch Reality

In our magnificent female quantum world—with neither time nor space in any sense recognizable today—what men call "natural laws" did not and could not exist. Even the term "natural law" is an oxymoron: nature, being female and therefore an-archic (law-less) and limitless, is the antithesis of the hierarchy and constraints that define male law. Because of this, men's assumptions about the nature of "nature," and the only way they are able to experience it on this planet, would have been unimaginable to us. Even their quantum physics, studied for years, can tell us little or nothing about how we lived in the reality of our own universe.

Femaleness *is* nature; it *is* the universe. We do not need to wonder how we adapted or fit into the scheme of things before the advent of men; we *were* the scheme of things.

The utter simplicity of this makes almost impossible now our trying to imagine how we and our lives might have appeared in that world. Having altogether different bodies and minds there, *being* the universe and all things in it, we were not subject to any of men's "natural laws"—to gravity, for example, or entropy, or Pauli's principle that two objects cannot occupy the same space at the same time. Instead, we could be anywhere and everywhere at once, could be not only our own unique selves fully and splendidly, but everyone else as well. We were without constraints of any description.

Being literally one, all beings of every species had constant access to the capabilities, energy, intelligence, experience and understanding of all others: of all stars and planets, of all animals, fish, birds, insects, and plants, of all oceans and mountains, of all trees, rivers, and rocks. Female consciousness was therefore prodigious and infinite, and our power total. Being female meant that we were each a world of boundless possibility, that there was nothing we did not know or understand, nothing we could not do or be. We did not *have* power, we *were* power.

Not only have we forgotten what power is, what it feels and looks like, but for a very long time we have been deliberately misled by the deluge of male-aggrandizing propaganda about it.

Twenty years ago, as I struggled to emancipate myself from some of the patriarchal assumptions ruling my life, I wrote in *Wildfire: Igniting the She/Volution* (p.83):

"Scrutinizing language has been part of [feminist theory] from the first. When we use language, we engage with symbol, the strongest magic. Feminists understand that one of the subterfuges by which men came to own the world was by appropriating this magic, embedding messages in it that justified their tyranny, and by so doing, changing the face of reality.

"Although we try to be cautious and on guard as we use their languages, they are so studded with word-mines that, if we are not careful, we find ourselves assuming that their sly, subliminal memos report the one and only possible world, and the one and only possible way to interpret and behave in that world.

"Such a classified memo is the word 'power,' another concept about which men have set the limits of feminist debate. We often end up trying to make distinctions between 'power-over' and 'power-to'—the latter seeming more peaceful, more cooperative, more womanly. But what we have rarely done is ask ourselves why we accepted any part of men's definition of power in the first place. Power is a confusing concept only if we assume that men have defined it disinterestedly.

"Nothing could be farther from the truth.

"I often hear feminists speak of 'the men in power,' and until recently used that phrase myself. But one day as I went to say it, it stuck in my throat.

"'Who says men have power?' a voice inside me demanded.

"'Why, *they* say so,' I answered.

"'Who benefits from the belief that what men say is power *is* power?' the voice insisted.

"'*They* benefit, of course,' I said.

"'A highly suspicious coincidence,' the voice mused."

In countless ways we have been conditioned to believe that power is what it most definitely is *not:* ruling countries, defeating other countries in war, enslaving people, owning corporations, getting elected, holding office, accumulating wealth, manipulating information, commanding natural resources—doing all the sadomasochistic things men have to do to continue to be on top, to own the world.

What this describes is not power but control, the opposite of power, quintessentially *not* power. But since men own the language, they can name their behavior whatever they wish, and what they most profoundly wish is that control *were* power because, though they long for power, control is all that is possible for them. Control is a manifestation of weakness, and because weakness begets violence, control is dangerous.

War, for instance, like rape, has its genesis not in power but in weakness. We learned this from bullies in grade school—one of the microcosms of patriarchal society.

Also, unlike genuine power, control is addictive and to fuel its rush must escalate rapidly. Because it never really feels like power—that is, can neither satisfy nor nourish, and ultimately reverts to emptiness—it can never be enough. Control and sadomasochism are synonymous, the mindset that drives powerless people to resort to greater and greater violence in an effort to fill the void, to feel strong and "on top"—often to feel anything at all.

All around us we see the havoc that control junkies have wreaked upon the world.

Understanding power more clearly now, I constantly re-program myself by refusing to say "the men in power." I speak of them as "the men in weakness": "the men in weakness today declared yet another war; the men in weakness are building more bombs, destroying more rainforests; the men in weakness today will rape at least ten thousand women." All this is evidence of personal and species-wide powerlessness and bully-dom (bully-dumb).

While the men in weakness are occupied with this "important" business, the women in power today all over the world—that is, the women on every farm, in every village and town and city—are seeing that everyone is fed and clothed, that the sick, the children, and the aged are cared for, that the sorrowing are comforted—a very short list of our massive life-sustaining, life-enhancing presence.

In short, in the face of men's rampaging greed and destructiveness, the women in power are struggling heroically to maintain the equilibrium of the world.

Femaleness is itself homeostasis and balance.

If what we have been conditioned to perceive as power is really only control and weakness, what is power?

Power is the generative, positive stuff of life, and because strength of character—integrity and equality (by definition impossible in patri- or any -archy)—is its source and its essence, it cannot destroy or limit or debase. Therefore, any hurtful behavior, any behavior that humiliates, causes pain or deprivation, or crushes health or happiness or hope is not power. Where there is power, there is *always* physical and emotional well-being and peace.

Women are and always have been the generative, positive, egalitarians of the world, the beings of power. This is why men have had to obfuscate and redefine power—and femaleness.

Though femaleness is the sole source of power in the universe, in perpetual terror for our lives over many millennia of violent male domination, we have hidden and denied it until we have nearly forgotten the truth of ourselves: that all female beings are power generators. The sun is female, giving and sustaining life. The moon and stars are female. The great oceans of all planets, the rivers and seas—all are female. The mountain ranges, forests, volcanoes, this planet and all planets, the females of all species throughout the universes—all these perpetually generate power and life.

But this is actually too small a definition; femaleness is infinitely more—and other—than this. Not merely generating and sustaining life, femaleness *is* life. It isn't only about loving, it *is* love. It doesn't just make equality and abundance possible, it *is* equality and abundance; it isn't just about brain intelligence, but about an infinite variety of intelligences that combine and recombine constantly in our every physical and spiritual atom. These are the very essence of femaleness, the metacore of us.

So when we talk about femaleness, we talk about all the power, all the intelligence there is, the wellspring of all the positive, healthful, joyful, abundance of life; when we talk about the female world we talk about the only possible paradigm other than patriarchy.

Typically, however, the eviscerated term "empowerment" is now used when speaking of women instead of "power"—the word with power. Empowerment, like religion, is an external application, some leader or someone outside ourselves "enabling" or "permitting" or "giving" or "teaching" us self-esteem, self-confidence, etc. These are good qualities to develop; so are all the others that such leaders and classes teach.

But the use of the term "empowerment" subliminally tells every woman who hears it—because language is symbol—that regardless of how strong and good we learn to feel about ourselves, these feelings are not power; it tells us that as women we are not inherently powerful—like men, who are seldom, if ever, recipients of "empowerment" efforts. It brainwashes us to continue to perceive ourselves and other females as needing external assistance—i.e., as powerless in ourselves.

As in almost every aspect of our lives, when we accept men's definitions/lies, without question—in this case that control is actually power—we re-program ourselves with the assumptions men have assiduously woven into the fabric of society to persuade us that women are negligible. Ironic, of course, since females are the *only* non-negligible, the *only* necessary, the *only* powerful beings in all the universes, even now when all understanding of true power has gone so deeply underground that we can hardly conceive of it.

I wish every woman who has influence with other women would begin talking about power, not "empowerment"; would talk about what power really is, how it is one-hundred percent female and beneficent. And go from there to studying, *right now, this minute*, what it looks like in our lives and manifests as beauty in the world; discovering that what men call power and what our lives as women prove it to be are diametric opposites; that instead, how what we feel, think, and do as females is what has always preserved life on this planet, how without female beings of all species, this and all other planets would be burned-out embers floating desolately in space.

And certainly not just because we have babies. Perhaps this least of all.

Forgetting every syllable men have spoken or written on the subject of gender—that's where we need to begin if we want to understand what femaleness is, if we want to believe in our truly immense power. Because the truth is that everything has always and will always depend for existence on female power; everything, every second, everywhere.

Fortunately, our power is limitless.

Since no one is able to imagine—has ever been able to imagine—a model of existence that is truly "other" in every respect from the belief system in which they have been steeped for lifetimes, we cannot begin to understand now what limitless personal power means. Profoundly entrenched in patriarchy, we automatically project men's worldview upon everything, all the time.

As do men, and, since maleness is the patriarchal mind, as they have since their beginnings. Early men's ability, therefore, to conceive of powerful entities—to create gods, whose mode of being was not nor ever could be possible for them—supports the hypothesis that they had to have actually observed such beings and that for centuries afterward carried their memory.

When maleness first befell the universe, every day in the full presence of the new arrivals, we demonstrated our inherent and limitless female power effortlessly in our every movement, with our every breath, and tried in every conceivable way to share it with the powerless newcomers. But because maleness is genetic powerlessness, we did not succeed then or ever could.

So the beings men observed, those with unlimited power, were women. From us came their dream of *men* for whom nothing was impossible; men, that is, with the power of women.

And so, out of their need for strong allies, out of their weakness and fear in our alien world, out of their innate reliance on external assistance, out of their envy of women whose powers they could never share, men created gods.

At first, needing male models that would "empower" them, they made their gods like them (except for having a broader arena for their exploits). Endowing them primarily with the paradigmatic characteristics of maleness, these gods were territorial, competitive, vain, sexually predatory, rapacious, violent, jealous, vindictive, and full of rage, bigotry (particularly misogyny), and destructiveness.

By projecting themselves upon these macho superheroes, men could envision themselves *en large,* be emboldened in battle, perceive themselves as stronger, better, more deserving than their enemies, and so sadomasochistically on and on.

But since it was clear from their beginning—certainly to us and at least unconsciously to them—that they would someday have an ending, the most important of all their gods' tasks was to save them from extinction.

In order to work this miracle of changing the very course of nature, gods were needed who were much stronger and more capable than their existing macho rough-drafts; for this they needed *saviors.* So gradually, men added to their gods' endowments the omniscience, omnipresence, and omnipotence they once had observed daily in women. By interjecting remembered evidences of our genuine power into the brutal repertoire of the superheroes, men finally upgraded and transformed male deity into a formidable final draft.

The significance of this for women is that since all that is positive about male gods is really men's memory of female power, by taking a cursory inventory of the benevolent powers men ascribed to their gods, we can extrapolate something of what it meant to be female before the advent of men and during patriarchy's beginnings. To become re-acquainted with ourselves, let's take a cursory inventory of the powers of the christian god.

Cursory Inventory: God ...

is not subject to any restrictions of time and space, so can be instantly anywhere and everywhere;

is not flesh and blood like humans; i.e., god is not a mammal (or a reptile, or a member of any other known species);

is not bound by gravity or any other "natural law";

can create matter out of energy—seemingly something out of nothing;

can walk on air and water;

can walk through walls;

can change water into wine;

can raise the dead;

can heal the sick;

can control the seas and elements;

can solve all problems;

has all knowledge;

always knows where everyone is;

always knows what everyone is thinking, feeling, and doing;

is everywhere, in everything—i.e., is omnipresent;

has unlimited creative powers;

is immortal—i.e., was never born, will never die;

is never ill, but always in perfect health;

is perfectly adjusted, has no personal or emotional problems (except for his necessary male characteristics);

does not need to sleep or eat;

was not created, but instead has always existed;

can be invisible;

can be non-molecular;

has more than five senses;

also has men's five senses but has them infinitely, being
  able to hear, feel, see, taste, and smell everything everywhere at once;

is multidimensional;

loves unconditionally, perpetually, and profoundly;

is not limited to any one planet or universe;

creates abundance simply by being.

And so on.

This magnificent being is men's unintentional tribute to
the females of their first memories. As a fictional hero, this
god reveals how men perceived and interpreted us when
they first arrived among us, how we looked in our power,
something of what it meant to be us. Though the cursory inventory is in no way complete, still it reveals us as stunningly
powerful.

Though men may have been able to reconstruct, at least
in part, what we did in our power, they could neither feel nor
understand our very different innerness, what we essentially
were: our spiritual grandeur, our intimate connection with every living thing, our total love for one another, the ecstasy
with which we lived our timeless lives.

Not possessing any of our qualities themselves, men overlooked them as sources of power and therefore did not ascribe
them to their gods. (Except, perhaps, to Jesus, whose reputa-
tion benefits greatly from men's memories of women's power:
the loaves and fishes, the walking on water, the healing of the
sick and the raising of the dead, the changing of water into
wine, etc. These appropriated female capabilities are innately
impossible to males.)

Some maintain, however, that the goddesses who came later offer us a better picture than men's gods of what we once were. Because we are always seeking to return to something we know and love but cannot formulate, the evidence that goddess cultures flourished in the deep past inspires us and gives us hope.

But before the advent of males, females were totally non-hierarchical in essence, neither needing gods nor capable of imagining them. We were each all the power there was. That a goddess culture emerged later is evidence, not of women's rising out of spiritual bondage, but of their finally succumbing to it. Goddesses were patriarchal women—hierarchical, ritualistic, religious. Sad echoes of their former selves.

So though goddesses were created and served for a long time, with some success, to preserve the truth that females had once been more powerful, the cultures in which they flourished were based on the male model of religion. The concept of deity, the word "goddess" itself, announces hierarchy, a way of being that is antithetical to femaleness and therefore impossible in the female universe. It is a religious—as opposed to a spiritual—concept

I have no wish to minimize the contribution that the goddesses of the world have made to our lives; I am glad of every positive model history can give us, every scrap of precious information about women—or even just supposition—that somehow survives the deadly patriarchal truth-shredder.

I realize that goddesses are global evidence of women's long courageous resistance against men's suppression, concealment, and erosion of female power. I know they are revelations of women's incredible dedication and effort over millennia to keep the truth of femaleness alive under the most ferocious occupation of their inner and outer environments, their bodies and minds. I am profoundly moved by this, and grateful.

But my memory and imagination combine to tell me that before maleness every female being was so much more powerful and so *other* than any goddess or god that has ever been envisioned that men's translation of us into their gods and women's translation of us into their goddesses still today can give us only faintest glimpses of our former selves.

Before patriarchy, religion would have been impossible to imagine: the need to perform, to "do" certain rituals as attempts to gather and enhance feelings perceived as "spiritual," the concept of external power—of worship, of sacrifice, of prayer—none of this would have made the least sense to us.

We would have been totally unable to imagine ritual, religion's universal language, bearing as it does all the male paradigmatic elements: it is hierarchical, requiring a leader; it is a means to an end external to itself, a stimulus designed to achieve a specific response; it is non-spontaneous and at least gently coercive, constraining those involved to participate as directed. In short, it is religion, not spirituality.

(Since every aspect of the male system is ritualistic, every woman ever born into patriarchy has suffered ritual abuse. Realizing this, we should not be surprised that many women will not participate in any overt ritual, even those devised and led by women.)

In the female universe, to be female was to be spiritual; femaleness *was* spirituality, not separate like a mantle to be put on or taken off, like ritual, but rather intrinsic, always present and spontaneously expressed in women and all female creatures. Our every feeling, our every move, our every breath—every aspect of our lives—was spirituality: our dazzling intelligence, our loving hearts, our never-failing trustworthiness. It was not something we had to *do* or needed to try to achieve or practice; it was not something that *could* be done or achieved. It was what each of us *was*, and what we were together. Spirituality was the essence of our power, our entire internal and external milieu.

But after all these long millennia of patriarchy, we no longer remember how to be spiritual any more than we remember how to be power. In women's circles, just as in churches, we have become accustomed to leaders and dependent upon them to use ritual to form us into some sort of coherent group. Women's creating rituals to celebrate femaleness, seeking consciously in this way to learn greater respect for themselves and one another, though to my mind the best religious experience possible is, nevertheless, still religion, not spirituality.

Now in global patriarchy, ritual is the most familiar way to think about and try to approach spirituality, individually as well as in groups. Religion is no longer foreign and unthinkable to women. As the successful displacer of spirituality, ritual/religion is now the norm.

This does not mean that women have stopped having spiritual feelings. We haven't, of course. Usually, however, such feelings are not subservient to our wills but arise spontaneously within us—and not often in the situations where they are "supposed" to, such as in church, or goddess circles. These feelings are much more common when we are, say, in the "forest church" or the "horseback church," or the "mountaintop church."

Like ritual, male rhetoric almost hopelessly confuses spirituality with religion, causing most people to think they are synonymous.

Take, for instance, the Toxic-Age men's perversion of the word "sacred," as in "the sacred feminine"—a term that connotes almost the opposite of what it denotes. Not only is the word "feminine" an egregiously misogynist male construct, but in patriarchy "sacred" has nothing to do with spirituality and everything to do with male egos, in every context referring to men and what they most fervently need and want. Those two words together tell us that acting "feminine"—i.e., focused on men and their well-being—is "sacred" because it is the way women most further men's interests.

When was the last time you heard "the sacred masculine" discussed? This term is not common parlance in the Toxic-Age movement because maleness is universally assumed—without the aid of hype or spin—to be intrinsically sacred.

So in our search for ourselves, we might take the word "sacred" as a warning that deliberate misdirection, if not out-right perfidy, is afoot. (It is *never* unintentional or merely fuzzy-mindedness.) Nothing in either mensworld or women's is "sacred" in any sense that men typically use the word. "Sacred" applies, as do all dichotomies, only in relation to its opposite—in this case, "profane". Since profane is all that is possible in patriarchy—where even life (or where *particularly* life, except of the unborn) is not sacred—no concept of "sacred" is relevant; in the female universe where all is sacred and can be nothing else, no concept of "sacred" is necessary.

One reason, among many, that women are so drawn to religion in this spiritual vacuum we call patriarchy is that godness is familiar to us. It calls to something deep within us for which we are desperately homesick—our own ancient SisterWitch selves. We know god-power is possible because we were (and deep down still are) this immortal power, this beyond-imagining goodness and glory.

Religion is men's substitute for spirituality, their effort to be powerful, as they once knew women to be—but without our power or feeling or understanding. Since men's life mode is one of doing, they try with religion to force spirituality to happen, but in trying to "do" it, are as unsuccessful as they are in trying to "do" power.

Like power, spirituality is inexorably innate. Inherent and existing in every atom of femaleness, it simply *is*. Outside of femaleness, it cannot exist, and there is no forcing it. (The use of the word "femaleness" as opposed to "femininity" is deliberate, since these are two opposite modes of being.) Religion is another of men's vain attempts to *do* what can only *be*.

Spirituality is not an activity, not something that can be made to happen with endless repetitions of mantras or prayers, or of tantric sex, or of looking to the "universe" for direction (the universe being just another term for the same tired old god who should have retired at birth), or of lighting candles, or of offering sacrifices, or of touching brows with holy water, or of bowing to the east, or of calling to the four directions, or of sermonizing, or of raising arms and keening, or of breaking and eating bread, or of handling snakes, or of singing.

(However, the shouting and singing, clapping and dancing of women in some African American churches in this country, and of women in some other cultures, is about as close as religion gets to spirituality right now on this earth. It is female [meaning powerful], egalitarian, and spontaneous.)

Unlike religion, spirituality is from the inside out, not from the outside in. Looking for it outside oneself is a sure way to find religion.

Spirituality is female, religion male, and they are antithetical, unable to exist in the same place at the same time. Spirituality, as an essential ingredient of power, is out of men's reach, and their substituting religion for it has not brought them any closer to it. One glance at their world tells us that *as a species* they are not honest or merciful or cooperative or peaceful—all spiritual qualities. One glance at their world tells us that although they may wear long dresses, conduct great sweat lodges, or talk a godly ("feminine") line, they have never been able to turn religion into spirituality, never been able to turn ritual into transcendence.

If women experience spiritual arousal in any ritual, it arises *despite* the ritual, out of our female souls, from what we ourselves innately are. Our great nostalgia for these feelings, for real spiritual connections, sometimes brings them to life for a few moments and gives us a glimpse of our former selves. When we are fortunate enough to experience them, we can assure ourselves, "If I could magnify this feeling a thousand-fold, then I would know a little of how I felt—who I was—every second of my life in the female world before patriarchy."

Women ask me how I could have been a mormon for so much of my life. Part of my answer is that I gave the church credit for the sweet feelings that sometimes came to me there.

Then for political reasons I attended mormon services for a few months after I was excommunicated and no longer a believer in either mormonism or god. Because I was unwilling any longer to do the work of bringing that delicious feeling up from my own soul and imposing it upon the proceedings, I was shocked at how empty, how boring and barren the service was; what a charade, what a pretense. I recognized that the source of my spiritual experiences there had never had anything to do with the *church* but everything to do with *me*, what I created for myself. I realized that my own female spirit had always overflowed and filled in the huge empty spaces left by religion, that the hollowness of men's church had forced me to be my own church.

Spirituality, like all else that is female, heals everything around it, enhances all life, brings abundance, peace, and unity. Religion, on the other hand, has not only never done anything of the sort, but is notorious for having had the opposite effect. Spirituality makes the world better; religion contributes hugely to making it worse.

Because they cannot be female or honestly demonstrate any of the positive female behaviors they attribute to god, men call them "miracles." Almost since their arrival, men have tried in every seductive and violent way they could think of to prevent us from being so ceaselessly and obviously miraculous, from putting them to shame simply by being female.

Still, despite their millennia-old, unceasing war against us, despite their every attempt to purge the world of our power, men have not been able to destroy it. Not by rape, not on the rack, not at the burning stake. Out of men's sight, women still fly, still walk through walls, still become invisible. One day soon we will regain our full power and far surpass every fictional deity ever created. Then out of our essence the female world will re-emerge, splendid and whole.

Despite having been supplanted briefly by the essence of maleness we call patriarchy, the whole of that fabulous lost female paradigm still exists all around and *in* women. It is what we most profoundly *are*.

This paradigm, this female world that is lying quiescent within us, has no creator—not universe, or great spirit, or god, or goddess. It is simply and gorgeously the external embodiment—the dramatization—of our femaleness. It comes from within all female beings, flowing out upon the worlds, flooding every atom with intimacy and peace, with all the blessings—all the resplendent *virtue*—of true power.

Women's world is more than home to us; it *is* us. Being that world, being in every way that universe, we need no governance but are perfect freedom.

Though females of all species are immortal—have lived forever and will live forever after males are gone—men's languages have no word for us; they have destroyed all memory of our former existence—except for their dazzling creation called god . . . and for our own memories and imaginations.

Since time is a transitory male illusion, and the truth is that everything exists and is present at once, right now then, high above the earth we lie singing in one another's arms, suffused with moonlight, gleaming with power, while the symphonies of the night sky stream around and through us.

Tonight, and through eons of nights to come, we are the music of the stars.

Chapter 6

The SisterWitch World of Being

Because our female world is not a time-based world of doing, the question is not, "What do we do in female worlds all day?" but rather, "How does it look to just be?" Would being be as boring as most people think?

Unfortunately, the timelessness of being cannot be rendered in words without contaminating it with doing, since doing is now the only way we can imagine anything happening at all, any way of living that is not totally inert and static. So though being is the least passive and the least boring of all possible modes, we imagine it to be lifeless and dull because it entails no sadomasochism, affords no rush of excitation, has no goal. Once again, we are unable to imagine it because it exists outside our present male paradigm.

Nevertheless, because being is limitless, we can try to imagine having no boundaries of any kind. For starters, in your mind's eye see yourself plunging into the ocean, sinking deeper and deeper, your body instantly, effortlessly adjusting. Imagine gliding through the velvet darkness of the underwater world, tickled and kissed by water creatures of every variety who then accompany you on your way, slipping under and over you, delicately touching you, happy to be with you.

Imagine suddenly being tossed about by the cross-currents your whale friends are creating as they weave and roll in the water below you in an intricate dance. Imagine yourself becoming a whale as you join them, your immense body cool and weightless, your nose and cheeks exploring their faces as you do-si-do, your heart exchanging glad tidings as you bow to your partners, your slippery sides sliding deliciously along their slippery sides. Imagine leaping together, all shining silver, high up into the sun, pirouetting gracefully before dropping back into the sea, flying again into the air and this time catching a wind current and sailing off together into the sky, full of vitality, loving your lives.

And singing for joy.

Imagine the vibration of that song as it comes roaring up out of your huge throat, reverberating along your spine, shaking you from nose to tail. Imagine the whole thunderous whale chorus as it rocks the ocean—and the heavens—and echoes poignantly back from whales in other seas on other planets in other galaxies. Imagine the delirious arousal of being part of this universal sisterhood of whales.

If females have no limitations, female whales—female *anythings*—have none either. Like us, they can converse with the moon and stars eye to eye up in the night sky. Trees and rocks are not bound to the earth, water is not a prisoner of gravity.

Femaleness means total freedom.

In the female universe, not only will we once again be able to experience the lives of hundreds of thousands of animal and bird and fish and insect species directly in dozens of ways we have not yet even tried to imagine—only one of which is that we can actually be them—but we also will also be able be all plants, experiencing their lives in all their complexity and beauty. Without making even a dent in our possibilities, we can live forever in the most intimate connection with the spirits, bodies, and minds of every marvelous female life in existence.

And with the souls and bodies of the million or so other women on this planet, touching and being touched—physically and spiritually—with a tenderness, honesty, and pleasure so exquisite that we now have no way to conceive of it, let alone express it.

Imagine being able not only to have your own feelings but other women's as well—all of them passionate, brilliant, full of fun and delight. Imagine being able to understand all they understand, perceive their exact perceptions. Imagine living each of their lives in addition to your own without the limitations and distortions of linear language. Imagine the global consciousness you share with every living thing (the rocks are alive); not just the expanded consciousness the Toxic-Age movement preaches but the ultimate consciousness it cannot begin to guess at.

Ho hum, you say. Is this *all?*

Well, though I cannot describe what being is or looks like, I can describe some of what it is *not* and does *not* look like.

To begin with, because being does not use anything, it cannot harm the environment. If you are a visitor to our world, you will not see anyone digging in the earth for any reason—tilling the soil or planting seeds or mining minerals or searching for water; you won't even see anyone walking on the ground. We would no more make holes in earth's skin or walk on it than we would desecrate our own or one another's bodies in these ways. Whatever riches lie within her body remain safe and free, contributing to the torrents of energy that stream from her to us and from our eternal springs back again to her, a constant energy exchange among us all—the stars and seas, creatures and plants—that keeps us balanced, strong, and intensely alive.

Have you been surprised to see us just suddenly appear—in a tree, in the sky, in the water near you as you swim? Being able to be instantly anywhere we wish to be, and not tyrannized by gravity, we do not scar the earth's skin with roads or paths. You've noticed that no telephone lines or electric wires or towers deface her landscape. We have no need for any, having instant communication (intimacy) with any organism in the universe, and loving the dark. It would not occur to us to try to lessen night's darkness; dark is what night is. We love its satiny richness, and see perfectly in it, even at the bottom of the sea or deep in the earth. Never having had enemies or been hurt in any way, we have no experience of evil to project into the dark and make us afraid of it. Dark does not mean "bad" to us and light does not mean "good." Light and dark are peers in every way, each perfect. Dichotomous thinking is not possible in our world.

You can search the galaxy over and never see a single being hunt, kill, or eat any other living being of any kind—not even cows eating grass. In a universe of infinite and instantly available energy, a universe where every form of life is female and constantly and effortlessly generating life energy, why would we ever need to murder another being for its energy?

Maleness will change all this when it lurches into existence. Parasitic, with no essential energy at all, males will prove an incalculable drain on female energy sources throughout the universe—the suns, planets, oceans, forests, mountains, and females of every species. As males greedily drain the energy out of everything around them without being able to replace even an ounce of it, women's bodies, devolving to adapt to men, will need to eat for fuel, too, as men do. And also because men, as well as cannibalizing animals and plants, will be gorging themselves on our energy every second of the day and night for the rest of their existence. Therefore, for several reasons needing outside sources of replenishment, we will finally have to give in and eat one another. In this, as in all destruction, males will lead the way, craving the flesh of other living beings, cannibals from their beginnings.

I say "eat one another" because we are all one here—literally, not metaphorically. Killing anything, therefore, would constitute suicide as well as murder, eating anything would be cannibalism. Though consuming and digesting other organisms is the least efficient possible way of producing energy, when energy-starved males appear on the scene, murder and cannibalism will come to be justified on the grounds of necessity. Males, the human doings, when their brief moment on this planet arrives, will gobble up resources with their every breath.

Being, on the other hand, needs nothing. As our guest, you will have noticed by now that we have no houses and need no clothing. This is because nothing can harm us. Our amazing bodies automatically adjust to remain comfortable, we neither need to cut down trees for fuel or shelter, nor to ravage other animals or plants for materials for clothing. The sun cannot burn us, the wind cannot freeze us. We are the sun and the wind, and they are us. We are peers with, and part of, every element of our universe, neither controlled by nor controlling anything.

(It is reported that Peace Pilgrim, who for many years walked the roads of this country encouraging people to work for peace, was able to adjust her temperature so that she needed to carry only a light jacket in all seasons. This was one of her female powers that survived from the pre-male world.)

Having total love and respect for ourselves—and since we *are* everything, this means having total love and respect for all life—harming ourselves or anyone else is simply unthinkable. Part of the reason for this is that in our female world we genuinely understand and are radiantly transparent to ourselves; we have no dim subconscious corridors full of repressed material that covertly sabotages our behavior and undermines our well-being. Nothing traumatic or negative lies hidden like a reef beneath the sea of our emotions waiting to re-break our hearts at the slightest touch, or cause us to strike out at anyone else.

That we know and love ourselves and all others unconditionally is a given, a female natural law. We live our entire lives surrounded by infinite love, to all of us from all of us. Experiencing nothing but joy, every one of us is forever safe from threat from any quarter; truly self-knowing and self-loving beings are incapable of doing harm, even unintentionally.

We would not be able to understand the concept of fear, never yet having experienced it for an instant. Look there! That deer at the lake's edge? See how at ease she is, how she is not constantly scanning the countryside or sniffing the air for danger. Have you noticed that there's a wolf rolling in the aura of the grass near her feet? I see that other creatures are gathering there, too, drawn by their desire for companionship and the luscious ambience of water. Here comes another deer, this one hurrying to catch up with the cougar ahead of her (several snakes move over to let her by), some turkeys, a couple of rabbits—all moving together effortlessly through the air. Also ducks nearby in the water, and a group of shining women, arms around shoulders and waists, walking across the lake toward them, just above the water.

A definition of being, then, might be: needing nothing, using nothing, doing nothing, harming nothing, controlling nothing. It means no work, no duty, no responsibility. Most difficult of all for the patriarchal mind to grasp is that the "being" world is without sadomasochism: no challenges, no achievements, no progress, no evolution, no pain or suffering; nothing to *do*—nothing to overcome or rise above or become, no lessons to learn, no goals to reach.

"But wait!" a woman's voice cries. "Don't take cooking away from me. It's my favorite thing. I love the whole process, from browsing through cookbooks, to finally serving delicious, healthful food to my friends at a beautifully laid table, watching them smile at their first taste. What would I do without it?"

Another voice says, "What I can't imagine is not being able to wander through aisles of gorgeous fabrics, all those colors and textures, dreaming of turning this rich blue velvety stuff—see, when you turn it to the light how subtly shot with purple it is?—into drapes or a bedspread, or a prom dress for my daughter. Or this! Here, touch it! As light and frothy as seafoam. Imagine it next to your skin as, say, a summer robe or a full midi-skirt swishing against your calves. Fabrics, the dreams they awaken, the creations they inspire—these have saved my life!'

"I'm a weaver!" protests another.

"A sculptor!"

"A poet!"

"A painter!"

"A writer!"

"A musician!"

All of them together in a chorus of complaint: "What about eating? Sleeping? Clothes? Houses? Art? How can we live without the very things that make life worth living?"

"I understand," I admit miserably. "How can I live without a book in my hands?"

I realize that I have failed, and cannot help but fail, to present the world of being as gorgeous and fascinating enough to vie with what we have created for ourselves here in our exile. Women, amazing beings that we are, have found thousands of ingenious ways of making life enjoyable even in patriarchy, the most wretched of exiles.

Because for so long we have been submerged in sadomasochism, because it is now the only paradigm we know, none of us in the entire universe at this moment can imagine the joys and wonders of the timeless female paradigm that existed forever before patriarchy, and that will exist forever after men are gone and forgotten.

In a sadomasochistic world, goodness cannot be made to appear even believable, to say nothing of interesting or desirable. If I have failed to make it so, so did Milton in "Paradise Lost." Lucifer, his complex, totally sadomasochistic—and therefore believable—fallen angel is a fascinating and sympathetic character, whereas god and Jesus—presumably the good guys—are lusterless and vapid, deserving of what they get simply because of their nerdiness. To men "goodness" not only seems unmanly, but also boring and a bit silly; too goody-goody, too lacking in conflict, in dark and dangerous plots, in excitation, hurt, pain, and grief; in competition, compromise, regret, redemption, forgiveness, etc.; in short, too devoid of sadomasochism.

Back in the days when I frequently gave talks at universities and conferences and festivals, my audiences consisted almost solely of women. But when I was campaigning for president, as many men as women showed up to hear me. I talked about the differences between men and women and why we needed to listen to women for a change. When I described what an enormous difference women's value system would make if injected into politics (I hardly need to point out how naive this was), men invariably pointed out during the Q and A how dull it sounded, how Pollyanna, how boring.

But cooperation and peace did not seem goody-goody to the women in those audiences; they did not find abundance, health, and joy either dull or boring. Instead they argued with the men, expressing the wish that all the world's inhabitants could experience these daily. The beauty and power of compassion, kindness, integrity—these did not bore the women then and do not bore most women now. As subject matter, virtues may be difficult to turn into patriarchal movies and books and songs, but to us they sound reasonable and familiar, the way any world should be.

So all I can offer—and I can promise this—is that, though every linear array of words, every attempt to describe with language the immense arousal of our spiritual, physical, and intellectual life in this female world only diminishes it, this world that we are is unimaginably thrilling, the very opposite of dull, static, and boring.

Our memories, our recurring dreams, our inchoate feelings from that world, soundly confirm this. Many and insistent—and becoming more so—they are bursting with such passionate, love-infused happiness that our sadomasochistically numbed-out hearts can barely sustain them.

They assure us that when we are home again we will never look back, never miss one single atom of mensworld; that being our original free and powerful selves, everything else in the universe will also be—finally, and once again in every way—exactly right.

PART III

Maleness and the Erasure of the SisterWitch Universe

Chapter 7

The Rule of the Retrograde

You ask, if women were so powerful, how did men come to control the world?

The answer is, without even trying.

Let us pretend that here we are, all women together in the female universe, powerful, alive and joyous beyond our present wildest imaginings, when suddenly a massive explosion rocks the universes. This is an explosion unlike anything we have known in all our eons of existence, an explosion that will turn our world inside out and upside down and bring untold misery upon us for millennia to come.

The Big Bang, genesis of maleness.

Until this moment, females have lived forever in a timeless, non-linear world; in fact, we *are* timelessness, infinite and seamless in all dimensions. Now, with the advent of maleness, though we may not recognize this immediately, our female mode of existence—"being," the source of our power—is profoundly threatened.

Also, along with its other alien accoutrements, the Big Bang has forced *time*, the linear plague that is male essence, upon our world, an aberration that will ultimately supplant the genuine power of femaleness and drive it underground for thousands of years. Requiring a vast timelessness, "being" cannot long survive the claustrophobic strictures of maleness.

Sometime after this monstrous explosion (who can possibly even guess how long?), our amazing, ageless bodies—strong, buoyant, and radiant with virtue and intelligence—begin to thicken, become dull and heavy, challenged by the denseness and weight of mammalian energy that now pervades the atmosphere of our planet.

At long last, a very strange thing appears among us: a puny, severely handicapped form of life that cannot sense or connect to anyone, unlike women who are so connected that we *are* everything. Now, here is a creature that remains locked in its own small brain and minute consciousness, unable to reach out or to be reached in the ways that are natural to us. Unable to understand the world around it, narcissistically aware only of its own terrible needs, bound to the ground, vulnerable, afraid.

These are men, the human doings.

For the first time ever, we experience pity, and with this condescension—this hierarchy, this sadomasochism—our minds begin to follow our bodies out of our anarchic world.

Immediately, we discover that these creatures with the strange growth at their loins do not generate the energy they need to sustain their own lives as we do. Instead, with their inborn and very strong energy vacuum, they must voraciously suck energy out of every female being around them—automatically, naturally, every second of their lives.

But even this astounding quantity of stolen life is not enough. Men's energy is so deficient as to be virtually non-existent. What we call "male energy" is really the vibration of their energy vacuum always running on high and at the same time, like a microwave, reversing female life energy, turning it into its deadly antithesis.

In addition, therefore, to incessantly grazing in others' energy fields, stealing and "using" their life resources, they must regularly take other life forms into their own bodies to obtain enough energy to survive. This killing and eating of others, this fateful introduction of murder and cannibalism into the female paradigm, destroys its innocence and integrity.

As well as rousing us to pity, their helplessness, their powerlessness, their total dependence creates a full-blown crisis. Matters rapidly reach a stage so desperate that we, whose "being" paradigm has had no concept of either "doing" or "using," are now forced into these modes by our efforts to help men survive.

To care for them, we also must enter deeply into time. Since they *are* time, their every cell infested with it—having a beginning and an end, existing inexorably along a continuum from birth to death—they cannot adapt to timelessness or any other given of our world, cannot live in any of the dimensions that are natural for us. Instead, since we are infinitely adaptable, to "save" them we move into *their* world of time and linearity and sadomasochism, the only dimensions in which they are able to exist and can be met.

From the outset, their helplessness demands our almost total focus, causing our ways gradually to be subsumed by theirs. In this alien world so completely opposite to ours, so restricted, so dull and inert, we begin to lose our power. We begin "doing" and "using."

We soon realize, for instance, that they cannot communicate with one another or anyone else in any way. Being an anomaly in our universe—so totally unrelated to and disconnected from anything else, their spirits so imprisoned within their bodies—they have no empathy about anything else: how it feels to be it, what inner life distinguishes it.

This is exactly the reverse of femaleness. Our female bodies live within our spirits, surrounded and permeated by oceans of spiritual power. Our spirits, therefore, free of all constraints, fill the universe, overlap, merge with every other spirit. This infinite consciousness, this communication via omnipresence, omnipotence, and omniscience—this is femaleness.

In the female paradigm, language is not only unnecessary for communication but would actively prevent it, make it totally impossible. Consequently, we have never even thought of it—until now.

Now, seeing that these creatures are not able to communicate as we do—by being everything, experiencing every living thing just as it experiences itself in all its diversity, wholeness, and richness; when we understand that, in fact, they have no way to communicate at all, we invent a way for them. Creating sounds that stand for objects and needs, we give them a spoken linear language.

But when we ourselves use it to communicate with them, we have to force our infinite reality into the narrow confines of brain cells, have to limit our consciousness and thought severely—almost totally, in fact—to make them fit into the puny vessels that are words. The more we use it, the more language imprisons our consciousness, preventing us from experiencing the world all at once in its multitude of dimensions. Linear, awkward, and small, demanding dependence upon weak brain cells almost exclusively, over time language drastically confines our consciousness, clogs our senses, stultifies us.

Now, thousands upon thousands of years later, language remains a hugely dis-unifying and intimacy-destroying disability for women, a weapon against our power. This makes language man's best friend.

But back to our earliest male-fraught days.

Despite our gift to them of language, men ironically cannot use it effectively to connect with one another or any of the beings around them. They remain as ignorant of and as non-attuned to the feelings and needs of anything outside them as ever. So we prepare *urims* and *thummins* for them—powerful oracular stones—to help them understand the world and their lives, to broaden their limited intelligence.

When even these do not improve matters, we accept the help of stones that volunteer themselves out of mountainsides and with them erect a perfect pyramid. In this—the first building in the world—we lay the pitiful new creatures in a stone bed positioned so that the most powerful stars in our universe, shining through a fissure in the ceiling, may pierce their deadened brains and spirits with life-giving energy. We hypothesize that this star-power will free them from whatever terrific constraints grip them, that it will restructure them and unlock their own energy and power.

But though we try this experiment again and again, the colossal energy cascade from the heavens has no discernible effect, and finally we discontinue it. We feel some ambivalence about this, however, because, though we are frantic to solve this first "problem," we are also troubled by our methods: they use our energy, the energy and material of the mountains, and the power from the stars; they force us to function according to a means-to-ends, stimulus-response, sadomasochistic model.

Despite trying everything we can think of to heal males' catastrophic inability to adapt to our world, and to forestall the untold damage we foresee if we fail, we do not recognize immediately that we are doomed to failure. Not only by men's genetic disposition, but also by our efforts: they move us inexorably out of our physical and spiritual habitat of femaleness.

Since large parts of our essence are our inclusiveness and limitless abilities, imagine our bewilderment when these marvelous assets become liabilities and begin to betray us. For instance, imagine our trying, first, to encompass maleness—to "be" what we do not recognize immediately as our antithesis, our nemesis. Then as we wake to the disastrous contradiction inherent in this, imagine our desperate attempts to maintain our wholeness and integrity while struggling *not* to encompass maleness.

Imagine the horror of finding that neither of these modes is possible for us now.

From this time forward, having in critical ways been catapulted into abrupt paradigm-shattering, consciousness-splitting disassociation from our natures, we are left feeling violated and confused; we who have always been so clear, so transparent and pure, now bearing shadows upon our psyches.

For millennia we try and fail to change men and for millennia we struggle against the consequent erosion of our power—of our Selves.

So when you ask how men, who were so weak and puny and vulnerable, originally took control of the world and have kept control ever since, I answer, "Through weakness."

As the story above illustrates, just by being their powerless selves, males instantly began to weaken the female paradigm and to establish their own. Though they could not generate energy, as mutations they were born knowing how to pirate ours, so that immediately upon arrival into a paradigm that had no concept of "using" or "consuming" anything or anyone, by their helplessness they introduced and established consumption as an imperative.

Thus they began their sojourn in our female world just as they would continue it for the next twenty-five to fifty thousand years or so: as parasites and consumers of all our powerful resources, physical, emotional, and spiritual.

Destined by their weakness to lay waste to Eden.

There was no active or conscious malice on their part in any of this, of course. If their species was to survive, they had no choice. They *still* have no choice. And they still have no consciousness of their perpetual theft of women's great gifts, are still unaware that as mutations they are completely dependent for life energy and creativity upon women and all that is female. This will be true for the rest of their existence and nothing can be done about it, any more than mosquitoes can be taught to reconsider sucking blood—bloodsuckers being what they most quintessentially *are*.

But they are no longer innocent. On some level—and often consciously—all males are aware of their species' malevolence toward females, and, knowing, collaborate in it one way or another, if only by doing nothing but being a carrier and a perpetuator of the plague of maleness.

In this brief synopsis of male beginnings appear the basic characteristics—instantaneous with the emergence of maleness—of the sadomasochistic male paradigm we now call patriarchy: linearity, inability to connect and adapt, parasitism (rapaciousness), and destructiveness.

An axiom that describes how this phenomenon takes control of all around it is "the retrograde rules," and it remains an integral aspect of our everyday lives in patriarchy.

Think of the disruptive kid in the class, for instance, who, because he either cannot or will not adapt, is really the one who controls the classroom, his behavior determining in large measure what is possible there.

The adults—teachers, principal, parents—typically spend a great deal of time trying to figure out how to deal with him, making lesson plans with his behavior in mind, coming up with strategies to alter or contain his intransigence. (In the case of men in general society, these strategies include governments, laws, religion.) His disruptive dominance forces everyone to put him first on their agenda, to adapt to him since he does not adapt to them, to focus on him to forestall his anger, his violence, his incipient mayhem. That is, to become obsessed with him.

This is how he controls everyone; this is the way he rules.

As a mutation—and therefore as a violent and destructive presence—maleness forces everything around it to change in order to survive its havoc-wreaking presence. Because males still cannot adapt but must continually use and destroy their environment—which includes all life—women are forced into perpetual reaction mode, constantly and unconsciously adapting our behavior, in our homes and everywhere else, to buffer theirs, to mitigate it, to try to keep it from destroying us and everything we love and value, everything we *are*.

Our necessary concentration upon them has altered us incalculably. In focusing upon them, we have been drawn into their sadomasochistic world and have become like them in many ways, disconnected from ourselves, from one another, and from the world that exists within us.

One way I keep in mind the now-alien reality of that female world is to remember something Jesse Raven Tree taught. She said that in large species such as humans, mutations are always retrogrades, the reason being that they are mirror images of femaleness, its direct opposite in every way.

Therefore, since femaleness is interdependence, mercy, empathy, peace, equality, unity, power—in fact, any quality that is life-giving, life-loving, and life-enhancing—it makes ugly sense that, as its mutational antithesis, maleness is parasitism, ruthlessness, violence, hierarchy, destructiveness, divisiveness, and hatred (to name a few)—all life-destroying characteristics.

(I deliberately use the word "femaleness" to differentiate between true female essence/power and women's transmogrification under men's rule. I have no illusions about individual women in patriarchy; I know that we are not all models of moral strength, kindness, and peace, that among us are many who imitate men's retrograde behavior. You know them: they squash our arousal with negativity and divisiveness, sucking our energy while giving back nothing life-sustaining.

Female obstructionists and trouble-mongers are an undoubtedly negative aspect of our reality, but they have one thing going for them: though they may be as divisive and controlling as men, they are *not* men; there is no genetic basis supporting their addiction to sadomasochism. Since their retrogradism is not innate, it is alterable—if they so choose. Maybe a few will so choose. But in the meantime, we must not mistake this behavior for femaleness or judge women as a species by those with this weakness.)

Out of genetic weakness, males use violence and terrorism to gain and keep control, sometimes subtly, sometimes blatantly. The rest of us try to survive this by focusing—no, by *riveting*—our attention on them, placating, pleading, helping, teaching, obeying, forgiving, loving; in short, by feeding them our energy and attention, by doing an immense amount of labor for them, and by conforming to their overt as well as their tacit rules for us.

However, being pleasant or tractable is also an essential part of the unconscious inborn strategy of male despotism, sealing as it does the pact between oppressed and oppressor known as the Stockholm Syndrome, a reality of every woman's life in patriarchy.

As a Stockholmed species worldwide, women adapt to men and to their system in the same ways that battered wives adapt to their unpredictable husbands (who bring them flowers after they've beat them up). And in these ways, constantly enable them.

This includes being consciously or unconsciously terrified of them. (Men are also terrified of men, knowing first-hand the demons that drive them.) Keeping this fear from rising into our awareness and destroying our precious and hard-won male-usions, denying the truth of their mutant and misogynist natures as it fairly shrieks at us nonstop from every side—daily this consumes much of our remaining energy and health.

Back in the days when I was doing lots of speaking, I often asked those women in my audience who were afraid of men to raise their hands. Typically, about a quarter did, a third or so sat quietly thinking about it, while the rest shook their heads and looked annoyed or protested to their neighbors or shouted aloud, "Not me!"

Then I'd give them a hypothetical situation:

"Imagine yourself in a big city walking down a dimly-lit street late at night. You have a long walk to your car through a deserted neighborhood, one that is strange to you. These circumstances make you uneasy, so you do your best to look strong and unafraid: you hold your head high, stride boldly and confidently toward your destination, grip your car keys with the longest key sticking out between the knuckles of your fist. You try in all the ways you know to reduce the likelihood of attack.

"Suddenly, you become aware of footsteps behind you. You assure yourself that this is nothing to worry about; after all, people live around here, and probably this is just one of them coming home.

"But the footsteps don't turn off anywhere, instead growing closer and louder. Beginning to panic, you pick up your pace. But the footsteps rapidly gain on you until you find yourself almost running. Then suddenly the person is nearly upon you, you can feel their presence, hear them breathing.

"With pounding heart, you clutch your key so hard it bites into your palm, swing wildly around to plunge it into his eye . . . and come face-to-face with a woman."

At that last word, everyone in the room exhales with relief. Why the relief if we're not afraid of men, all of us? And why be ashamed to admit it? Not to be afraid—actually, on some level not to be terrified—is dangerous. Males are truly fearsome, the only creatures in the world that are.

None of which means that we should let fear stop us from living our lives as richly and joyously as we can in their midst, but only that we need to remember a very important truth: men are genetic rapists—of our bodies, of our ideas, of our energy, of all the resources of the world—and on some level every woman in the world knows it.

(After using this story one night in a speech, someone told me that Robin Morgan had used a similar example in one of her books. I hadn't read that book, but I still want to give Robin credit for also having the idea.)

If we are interested in understanding our history, we might want to think about the genesis of our fear of men and our consequent ages-long preoccupation—our *obsession*—with them, how profoundly over untold centuries it has changed us, how to this day it continues to dominate and imprison us, and how it prevents us from being our real Selves.

But if we are not our real Selves, who are we?

Though the creatures we have all become since men's advent are certainly not male, neither do they even approximate fully-realized female. Since there is no language for this disturbing not-ourSelfness, no slot for us in men's strictly dichotomous catalog of possible beings, we essentially have no reality; have in their world no meaning, no genuine existence. Trapped in this murky limbo, we are also unclear and confused about ourselves.

But not for much longer.

In the meantime, women worldwide are eagerly awaiting a new world, many unfortunately looking to men to be their partners in creating it. But maleness will play out its genetic drama no matter what any of us hopes or believes about gender or about men; their doom cannot be changed, put off, or diverted. It is what they are, not something that is arbitrarily happening to them or vindictively being done to them: they *are* linear time, they are beginnings and—in keeping with their essence—they are endings. They will not be in the universe in any form when their allotted time is up but will be truly extinct, never to be seen again.

As some Native American and Australian Aboriginal women have known from time immemorial, mutations are short lived; it is one of their chief identifying characteristics.

Though males, as a species, have always had to work hard to feel, now, near their end, they will require even more violence to feel anything at all; it is the fate of sadomasochists that ultimately no amount of mayhem will suffice. My hope is that men disappear before they destroy the planet and all life in an attempt to achieve one last vast and fiery orgasm.

Women who cannot bear the thought of men's extinction may choose to follow them out of existence rather than survive into a male-free world. I believe that, for lots of reasons, many women—perhaps most—will reject the approaching female world and will disappear with men. Some of them will be the women who are unable to imagine living without men—even to imagine *wanting* to live without them (we have become deeply attached to our oppressors); others, unable to believe that they can live outside the sadomasochistic paradigm, will fear losing this refuge—i.e., their access to the addictive rush of illusory superiority and control that they perceive as life. And millions of others who, as men have taught them, profoundly hate women and are repulsed by the idea of a woman-only world.

But those of us whose most ardent dream for thousands of years has been to live free of sadomasochism and all that that entails—how could we not stay around to dream that dream into being? Why would we think of missing even one second of the immeasurable peace and joy of a world without retrogrades?

So you can be absolutely certain that when once again all is female, you will find us SisterWitches here, fully alive at last and spilling over with joy.

ॐ ॐ ॐ

On the mirror of Lisa Garrett's bathroom in Asheville, North Carolina, I first read this excerpt from the writings of Arundhati Roy:

"Another world is not only possible, she's on her way. Maybe many of us won't be here to greet her, but on a quiet day, if I listen carefully, I can hear her breathing." (In "Come September," War Talk, South End Press, Boston, MA, 2003, p. 75.)

Another world *is* on her way, and without doubt many of us will be able to keep our promise to be here to greet her. What we may not have understood when we made that promise—or maybe we did!—is that she is not separate from us: we *are* this fabled other world. As soon as maleness is gone, she will emerge from us, her wonder unsullied, her power undiminished.

We need to be here for this.

But friends shake their heads disbelievingly and say, "You know very well that women are riddled with patriarchy; that, in fact, we have become very like men, believing what they believe (and sometimes more so), acting as they act. Patriarchy—sadomasochism as you call it—has become such a part of us and has so corrupted our femaleness that it will take a lifetime, maybe even several lifetimes, for us to deprogram ourselves of it."

On the contrary, my friends, we do not have to worry about this at all. Maleness is not only, or perhaps not even primarily, a genetic presence. It is essentially a female-mirror-image possibility—a mutant and unnatural presence—in the energy of the universe. As is true of all mutations, its ability to perpetuate this presence, to maintain itself as this energetic possibility, is limited by time and entropy. When its time runs out and it disappears forever as a possibility, maleness will disappear from everywhere at once—even from what seem to us to be unbreachable citadels: our hearts and minds.

When this happens, we will not have to spend two seconds either de- or re-programming ourselves, or trying to figure out what to do next: "seconds" and "next" and all other time-bound concepts will no longer exist. Patriarchy—men's values, their systems, their ways of viewing and behaving in the world—will fall from us like the wretchedly-fitting worldview it has been for us from the start. Instantly, every atom of us and of the world will be free of it. When maleness goes, it really will be gone, not a vestige remaining.

On that glorious day, without even having to think about it, we will be again the beings we truly are. Effortlessly, we will take up our lives where they were interrupted thousands of years ago by a gigantic explosion that rocked the universe with evil.

❧ ❧ ❧

Chapter 8

The Good Man

When we tell the truth about men in order to understand our own lives, some woman always protests, "Well, not all men are like that! My husband (boyfriend, father, brother, son) is an exceptional man. I'm really lucky to have one of the good ones." What the "exceptional" defense actually demonstrates, however, is how surely women accept that men in general are bad, as evidenced by the disclaimer that their male person is an *exception*, a *good* man, unlike the others. The good man is the exception that proves the rule.

In addition, if she refuses to believe that men are morally and spiritually deficient as a species, then she can relax back into the comfortable illusion that there are idiosyncratic reasons for the behavior of every bad man. She is the same woman who misses the entire point and insists, "Women are just as bad!" a ploy that allows her to deny that genetics plays any part.

It is true that some men have taken great pains to keep their male tendencies in check, or were born with low levels of testosterone and libido, and consequently behave less like retrogrades than others. It is also true that some women seem almost to have become male. But the crucial difference is that men are genetically male—that y chromosome simply cannot be ignored.

Certainly in patriarchy all men benefit from the mutant behavior of "bad" men; and they are all aware somewhere in their souls that they first obtained and now keep male privilege only through the acts of terrorism these "bad" guys daily perpetrate against females: rape, incest, battery, degradation, torture, murder, sexual slavery, unpaid labor, assault, poverty, pornography, enforced marriage and motherhood, genital mutilation, widow burning, prostitution, job discrimination, discrimination in every facet of society. (These are just the obvious, overt weapons and do not include any of the dozens of subtly soul-destroying ones, such as condescension and guilt.)

These acts don't just happen. They are as much institutions of patriarchy as governments, churches, schools, economic exchanges. They are patriarchy's superstructure, its definition, all absolutely essential to keeping women emotionally and physically enslaved. All absolutely essential for male supremacy.

And so the atrocities in the fathers' war against women go on and on, and the "good" men do nothing.

But I don't understand. How can they be good and still turn their backs on the massive violence against half of what is inaccurately deemed "the human race"? What does "good" mean if it doesn't include trying to stop atrocities against the women they say they love? If this is "good," what is "evil"?

"Good" men turn blind eyes because they know they have to. They know that incalculable violence against female bodies and spirits is necessary—every second of every day—in order for men to keep privilege and control. All men know it, men of every race, class, sect, and sort. It is their common denominator and unbreakable bond across all cultures and planets.

So the "good" man realizes on some level that he must—if he wishes to maintain his group's supremacy (and for men not to be "on top" in all ways, not to control the world, is unthinkable even to him)—encourage and support with his silence and inaction the countless large and small, physical and psychic wounds his fellows inflict on females to keep them on the bottom and men on top. This renders his own silence and inaction as central to the continuation of the war against women as any acts of the bad guys.

If the definition of a "good" man is that he cares deeply enough about the females in his life—his mother, sisters, wife, daughters—to use his male privilege, money, connections, and varied resources to try to mitigate in some way this incessant, no-holds-barred attack on them, how many "good" men would you say you know?

I'd like to ask the women who perceive the men in their lives as "good"—in this way denying that maleness is in itself women's deadliest danger—what any one of their particular "good" men is doing to stop this destruction of her and her species.

Is he gathering the men in audiences to walk every unescorted woman to her car after concerts and plays? Or organizing groups of "good" men to appear after every performance, at the end of every workday in the underground car parks, in the parking lots day and night of every mall, every large store, all bars and clubs, on the jogging and hiking trails, to protect women from rape, torture, and murder?

Has their "good" man given up his full-time job for part-time work that will allow him more time to do this critical work of love and peace? Is he actively trying to get men to stop raping and beating, terrorizing and killing their wives and daughters, girlfriends, prostitutes; is he is rallying public opinion against these behaviors, trying to persuade men that taking a female life is as heinous as taking a human life?

Surely, at the very least, he is lobbying his employers or his corporate board to hire women and pay them what they are paying men for doing the same job. It goes without saying that he is talking to his male friends in various businesses about this small step of demonstrating respect and concern for the women in their lives.

Isn't he?

No? You say he is doing nothing of the sort, but that that doesn't matter because he's so nice to you?

Thirty years ago I had a private audience with Gordon Hinckley, the man who currently heads the mormon church and who covertly headed it then when it was organizing members against the ERA. Defending the actual, albeit non-functioning, president whose decision the anti-ERA policy was purported to be and who I had just accused of profoundest misogyny, Gordon retorted pompously: "He has done more for the women of this world than any living man!"

"Such as what?" I asked quietly.

Accustomed to being believed without question no matter how absurd his statements, he hemmed and hawed, giggled—since then I always refer to him as "giggling Gordie"—swung around in his desk chair several times, examined the ceiling as if the right answer might miraculously appear there, and finally blustered, "Well, he treats his wife so well!"

I was too disgusted even to laugh.

I know that many men whom women count among the "good" ones are actually indistinguishable from the bad ones except that they are better actors, and I truly believe that if women could be inside their "good" man's consciousness for just a day or two, they would be sick with disillusionment. Men have learned what they have to say and how they have to act to get the energy from women they must have to exist. Aside from this play-acting, they have scanty selves—hollow men, walking spiritual wastelands.

Because men have erased from our memories all knowledge of what femaleness truly is, and have brain-washed us into believing that men and women are essentially the same, women project upon these empty men-husks our own gorgeous richness of consciousness, our own lush inner landscapes, our own goodness and moral grandeur, and consequently perceive and interpret men as possessing them just as we do.

And men—having to try to live up to this, having to speak and to try to act as if they are loving, caring beings, having to make women believe they have the same values in order to get their respect and to use their energy, time, bodies, and labor—have also nearly convinced themselves that they actually feel the feelings they are so able to pretend, so able to describe in speech and translate into facial expressions and body language. Though most of them at various times are at least vaguely aware of their dissembling and manipulation, they feel no compunction about it; it is, after all, necessary for survival, and so habitual as to pass largely outside their notice.

Their lack of consciousness of what they really feel reminds me of the phenomenon experienced by a myriad of women who have never had an orgasm during sexual intercourse but who, from having acted it out so many hundreds of times, firmly believe they have.

How do we know they haven't? Years ago a woman professor told me about her long-term research into women's faking of sexual pleasure. One hundred percent of her sample admitted to faking pleasure: moaning at appropriate moments, or saying, "yes!" or "oh, that feels so good!" when they weren't really enjoying the experience much or at all; and, as she had expected, lots of them *consciously* faked orgasm.

Her big surprise came when a significant number of her subjects, thinking about it for the first time and checking out their subsequent sexual experiences, realized that for their entire sexually-active lives they had faked orgasm without being aware of it.

In this same way, over many thousands of years, most men have convinced themselves that they are caring beings by putting on the empathetic, loving expression, by feigning the correctly sincere tone of voice, and by saying the right words—that is, by mimicking women. But being great pretenders does not make genuinely moral, non-hierarchical, peaceful beings.

So although men have become consummate mimics of women's feelings, their true innerness bears no resemblance to ours. For proof of this we need only look at the world they have made out of the deepest desires and the grandest, noblest impulses of their souls: a desolate, blood-soaked battlefield, a huge physical and spiritual garbage dump.

But to give the occasional "better" man his due—the one who has succeeded in acting more like women than others: one reason he does not actually do anything to try to hold back the tidal wave of violence against females is that he knows it will do no good. Yes, he can struggle daily with some success to manage his own prurience and sadism, but he can stop neither his own nor his brothers' perpetual unconscious vampiring of female energy. Maleness is a parasite of unfathomably massive and destructive proportions. This is its nature and it cannot be changed.

As women, we know this whether we want to acknowledge it to ourselves or not. Partial proof of women's deep knowing is our current plague of anxiety, despair, fatigue, ill health, untimely deaths. It takes the strength out of our bones to realize that despite our thousands of years of loving men and trying with all our strength to turn them into truly moral beings, we have not changed male nature one iota, and in trying have given away and used up nearly all our energy.

If nothing can be done about them, why talk about men at all?

We talk about our lives on this planet with men because truth has great power; to face and internalize it gives us immense inner strength and courage; to tell it openly ennobles us.

Truth has such power, in fact, that to tell even the slightest portion of truth about men is the most profound of all taboos in mensworld. Throughout patriarchy, women speaking against men have brought terrible repercussions not only upon themselves but also upon the rest of us. This explains why, to keep the rest of us from breaking this taboo, frightened women always step forward and haul out that predictable, shopworn couple, the "good" man and the "bad" woman. This threat is real, the terror justified. Not only does it cause us to deny men's behavior but also to fear one another's possible responses to it. We therefore police one another, scoff at any truth that's told, belittle or dismiss dangerous philosophies such as feminism—and stalwartly defend the "good" men among us.

Chapter 9

Telling the Truth

From Pilate's mocking question, "What is truth?" we can infer that truth has been slippery for a very long time. Of course it has; men make it up as they go along, calling truth whatever expedites their machinations *du jour*. They have also amassed a seemingly endless repertoire of other sleight-of-mind tricks for turning it completely inside-out and upside-down. These ploys to disguise and conceal the truth make Pilate's question to the crowd as relevant now as it was the day he (presumably) asked it 2000 years ago.

Or maybe even more so. Truth has never been a standard in patriarchy but now, like men themselves, it has become a seriously endangered species. Just during our lifetimes it has been degraded almost to the point of comedy by being applied to such public statements as: "I was in such shock I couldn't try to rescue her from the river or go for help," "I am not a crook," and "Arab terrorists master-minded the attack on the World Trade Center."

Greatly abetting this general obfuscation, the Toxic-Agers continue to encourage each of us to claim our own personal truth about every subject, as in, "That may be *your* truth but it isn't *mine.*

During my years of meeting with groups of women around the country, I occasionally mentioned rape as an example of men's violence against women. Almost every time I did, some woman would respond, "Well, no man has ever raped *me!*" Rape, despite being pandemic in mensworld, could not be *the* truth because it was not *her* truth. The implication is not only that *her* truth supersedes *the* truth, but that *the* truth does not even exist.

This concept has rendered truth so legion that we are fairly drowning in the millions of one another's wildly contradictory "truths." In this and scores of other ways men have so splintered and buried and diluted truth that it has nearly ceased to be a quality or measure of factual reality. That suits men just fine. The more obscure it becomes—preferably to the point of total invisibility—the more freedom they have to run the world as ruthlessly as they wish.

To erase the truth as completely as possible is the entire purpose of patriarchal programming, the institutionalized system of male-aggrandizing lies that masquerades as truth worldwide. This perpetual disinformation machinery is the source of men's most sophisticated and profound contradictors of the truth. Purporting to be exegeses of every aspect of life, its lies are unquestioningly believed by most of the world's inhabitants and dictate almost all behavior.

So although *the* truth still exists around us everywhere every minute, we have assimilated our programming so thoroughly that only a very powerful desire to see the truth can allow us any glimpse of it at all. To awaken women to the truth of their condition has been the work of feminists all through history.

But many women, perhaps even most, do not really want to wake up. Their programming and the many lovely illusions it generates reassures them continually that they are in the right place doing the right things. Wanting to be accepted, to be safe from emotional and financial deprivation, *not to suffer*, they have little incentive to upset the status quo. So for the most part they do not care whether conventional "truths" are really true or not. In addition, their intuition warns them that too close an examination could calamitously disrupt their equilibrium and the rhythm of their relationships and lives.

(They are right, of course. This is precisely what happened to millions of us: we had massive heart attacks called "feminist awakenings." Feminism is dangerous in just the ways women fear, and in many they do not know enough to fear. But personally I have never regretted losing any of my illusions because of embracing it and if I had it to do again, would simply do it a whole lot sooner.)

In the last quarter century in this country, many women's unwillingness to deal with the truth has had to do with the widely-held Toxic-Age superstition that talking about something makes it happen; that, for instance, the negative energy of acknowledging men's undesirable behavior actually *causes* it.

I spoke in the California woods once at a women's camp where those who attended were mostly Toxic-Age goddess-worshipping women with little or no feminist consciousness. In the course of trying to remedy this lack a little, I mentioned rape and incest and general all-out war against women as some of men's most necessary work in keeping patriarchy up and running.

You would have thought I'd dropped a bomb; actually, I guess I had. Women began moaning, then leaping and screaming and fainting out of the audience to the nearby river, there to be ministered to by one another, prayed over, and bathed to cleanse themselves of my negativity. My endangering everyone by saying the words aloud was felt to be the cause of these anxiety attacks, not men's behavior; not the fury every woman on the planet harbors toward men and, out of unacknowledged fear, spends oceans of time and energy trying to deny and control.

When the river exorcism was finally over, a large group of these now-shriven women surrounded me and for over an hour castigated me for perpetuating men's outrages— by talking about them!

Although their twisted-faced, displaced rage was alarming to behold, it didn't persuade me I had done anything wrong; that hadn't been the intent of their assault anyway. They actually got exactly what they wanted: a huge sadomasochistic rush from telling me everything they found despicable about me. They left feeling exhilarated, their faces glowing with righteousness.

But most importantly, they left feeling safe. Having defended men against the truth, having proved their loyalty to men, clearly having taken men's side against the enemy, they had paid another week's rent on men's approval and restraint.

Being anti-feminists, however (meaning opposed to learning the truth of their condition), they didn't recognize that the degree to which they felt defensive on men's behalf that day was the degree to which men had enslaved them.

Neither did they realize what you and I have known for a very long time: nothing women do for men will render us safe from them—for a month, a day, or an hour. The anger toward feminists harbored by women such as those at the California camp masks their terrifying (albeit unconscious) memories of what men have done to *all of us* when *any of us* told the truth about them.

They also forget that for many thousands of years before feminism, men's all-out war against women raged across the planet despite hardly being mentioned.

Take, for instance, the centuries-long ritual torture and burning alive of nine million European women in the most public places of every village and city, including London. Where can we find this massacre seriously portrayed (that is, verified, borne witness to) in Shakespeare's work, for instance, or in that of any other European writer or reporter or artist between the fourteenth and seventeenth centuries, the witch-burning times men so tellingly, so ironically, call their "Renaissance?"

Or, perhaps *not* ironically. Exterminating millions of powerful women effectively destroyed almost all dissident energy on the European continent, leaving the inflation of men's egos unobstructed by reality, and men free to exploit all remaining female energy without resistance. Good timing for a male renaissance, I'd say, and clearly not just coincidence.

That last great purge, that massive attempt to break women's mind and spirits once and for all, succeeded in so compounding our Stockholming that it almost destroyed our connection to one another, the connection that was, and is, our power. It also came within a hair's breadth of erasing women's painstakingly guarded secret knowledge and history from global female consciousness.

Western women endured the four hundred years following this holocaust in the deep paralytic silence of terror. Slowly the shock subsided and we rallied, took up the campaign for suffrage, and initiated the movement for women's liberation. The Women's Movement flourished.

Then waned.

Now silence hangs over the earth again, an eerie, unsettling silence surrounding women's subjugation. This is understandable. We live in a time so perilous that we hardly dare look at our danger even out of the corner of our minds. The energy of being always under threat of annihilation feels, when we dare allow ourselves to feel it, far too like that of the Burning Times.

Then we read in the newspaper that our state educational association again this year is considering seriously the proposal to ban "Frosty the Snowman" from the schools. Why?

Because it is about witchcraft. You remember: *There must have been some magic in that old silk hat they found, for when they put it on his head he began to dance around.*

Seeing in print that men's fear of women's power is still seething beneath the surface and boiling up again here and there across the land chills us. We shiver and hunker down deeper into our disguise of "normalcy." Even if we do not consciously see such evidences, our radars are honed to super-sharp acuity by past traumas at men's hands, and we sense that women everywhere are in terrible danger.

So we shut up. Because in this atmosphere, to speak the truth of women's lives seems lunatic. Also (using rape as the metaphor for all men's violence against us) we realize that men rape us if we tell the truth about rape and rape us if we do not, so why risk talking about it anymore?

Certainly not to try to change men's rapacious behavior; nothing can ever succeed in stopping or even slowing that down. Genetically, men were rapists from the moment they appeared in this universe and, despite females' unceasing efforts to change them, will go out of it rapists still. So after thousands of years of unsuccessful effort, it makes sense to stop trying.

We talk about rape to remind ourselves to be steadfast in refusing society's almost overwhelming imperative to blame it upon women. We tell the truth about rape to remind ourselves that we and all women everywhere are one-hundred percent innocent of any wrongdoing deserving of men's violence toward us.

Also, telling the truth that rape had been men's universal mode since their beginnings can encourage us to extrapolate the future from the past 25,000 to 50,000 rape-driven, rape-saturated years of men's reign and to withdraw our trust from them now, before it is too late to escape the fire; to dare read the clear signs of their escalating fear and hatred of females and get out of their way.

In their never-ceasing war against women, one of the most diabolical (because most effective) of men's ploys to divert our attention from the truth is to lay the blame—not just for the rape they *call* rape, but for all their nefarious destructiveness—upon women, constantly adding to our already disabling burden of guilt, worthlessness, and self-hatred.

Over the last two decades, I have heard countless women bemoan, for instance, that "we're destroying the ozone layer!" or "we're destroying the planet!" Surprised, I ask them how they are doing this. Do they and their women friends get together and plan how to make and sell more atmosphere-killing automobiles? Do they band together to massacre more forests, rivers, and oceans? No? Then why are they so eager to implicate themselves?

Because it exonerates men *as a species*. Most women, literally Stockholmed out of their minds, believe everything men tell them. Men know and capitalize upon this. For instance, as part of training women to share the blame (and even to take it all), male scientists, newscasters, and writers of books invariably report that "we are killing the oceans," and "we are destroying the environment," the word "we" blaming all this destruction as equally on women as on men. Men do not even consider telling the truth: "We men, and we men alone, are guilty of destroying this planet."

Women take the blame, not only because men say so, but also because it relieves them of the necessity of facing the truth. In this way, they maintain their illusions of a safe world inhabited by "good" men, people just like themselves only with penises.

How could they bear to face even the simple truth that all destruction of the natural world is conceived and carried out by males—their sons, brothers, fathers, husbands, friends? The implications of this could swirl out through their entire lives, like the ripples on the proverbial pond when a stone is cast into it. Except in this case with the power to rip their lives apart.

Rather than risk toppling the shaky world they are so carefully holding together, they take the blame themselves.

They take the blame also because they truly believe they are at fault. The lies of patriarchal conditioning have led them to accept that men do what they do because women have been remiss in some way—in particular that mothers have failed to teach their sons to be good men. Thus, men are not to blame for anything; all is the fault of their unloving or negligent mothers. Once, briefly, the most honored of all humans, mothers now have become the lowest of the low, responsible for all evil largely because they do not stop men from doing it.

This basic patriarchal principle of blaming women for all men's evil is the gospel for billions of people, including most women. Ironically, its very universality is the most telling evidence that it is conditioning, not truth; anything most people believe is almost never the truth, almost always conditioning.

Another way men transfer the blame from themselves to us, is to insist that no one and nothing outside us can "make" us feel anything that is not already part of our psyches. In this they have taken an atom of truth and turned it into a Mt. Everest-sized defense of male behavior.

In maintaining that we are totally responsible for all our feelings, that their origin is within us and not caused by anyone else's behavior, men contradict themselves yet again. As psychologists, they assure us that the traumas we suffered in our early lives at the hands of other people *cause* us now to feel worthless and guilty, unable to sustain intimacy or joy. Helping people discover what the traumatic experiences were that presumably *caused* these feelings and helping them do something about them is the basis of patriarchal therapy.

But when it comes to women's pointing out to men the grief their treatment *causes* us—whoops, suddenly our feelings have no basis in anyone else's behavior. "If you'll just look honestly inside yourself," they say, "you'll see that your reactions have nothing to do with *us;* they're all about *you!*"

We can see more clearly what utter nonsense this is if we look at any oppressed group *other* than the global caste of invisibly oppressed people called women. If, for example, we listen to the feelings of members of groups that are oppressed more visibly (because half of them are men), groups that suffer discrimination for reasons of race, or class, or nationality, for instance, we would agree that they are caused by the injustice and harm they have experienced at others' hands. In their situation these feelings are clearly justifiable, even unavoidable, and certainly not merely projections of their own idiosyncratic problems or pathologies.

But when it comes to women, solely as females—not as persons of color or of the working class or of any other oppressed group—if we talk about how men's hatred of women has caused us almost irreparable damage, we suddenly become man-haters and therefore to be instantly disbelieved and scorned.

This "patriarchal reversal," as Mary Daly so brilliantly terms it (in *Gyn/Ecology: the Metaethics of Feminism*, Beacon Press: Boston, 1978, pp. 8, 139, etc.), constantly erases the fact that what women face and struggle against every second of every day is not our hatred of *men*, but men's hatred of *us*, and that the way this hatred is vented upon us—rape and incest, for instance—does indeed *cause* us to experience serious emotional trauma and upheaval, often for the duration of our lives.

One significant reason many women do not want to be associated with feminists is that, thanks to this topsy-turvy view of the "truth," feminists are assumed to be man-haters. Not only here, on the brink of the extinction of men and their world; not only now, when men are generally more terrified and dangerously off balance than ever before in their history; but all through history, for a woman to be thought a man-hater was for her to be in deadly peril.

For anyone to believe, however, that hatred of the sort men harbor toward women is even possible for women *as a species* to feel toward men is to misunderstand femaleness completely. Anger, rage, fury, grief, madness—these are appropriate responses to men's abuse, and as such signify something very different from hatred.

Anyone who thinks feminists hate men needs to learn what hatred looks like. This is easy, requiring only a brief study of male behavior. Hatred is what propels men—every second of every day everywhere in the universe—wantonly, ruthlessly, and in a myriad of merciless ways, to destroy all that is beneficent and life-sustaining, all that is beautiful and good.

All, that is, that is female.

While they are busy at this, however, women *as a species* display no systematic behavior toward them in return that could possibly be construed as hateful. We do not rape them by the hundreds of thousands world-wide every day, we do not sell them into sexual slavery by the millions, we do not murder and torture them for the thrill of it, or for any reason whatever—though in patriarchal terms, we would be more than justified in doing so. We do not deprive them of their human and civil rights, or purposefully impoverish them. The worst we do *as a species* is tell the truth about them.

Men's violent expression of their woman-hatred is therefore *not* an appropriate response to our treatment of them. In fact, since men are our children, we have loved them and done all we could to help them flourish. And despite overwhelming evidence of men's hatred of us, to this day most women continue to love men as near to unconditionally as is possible on earth.

Saying that in general women are constitutionally unable to hate men as they hate us is not to imply, of course, that our only alternative is to love them. A huge number of women in this world appropriately and thoroughly dislike and distrust them.

Prepped by the Toxic-Age fathers, someone is sure to suggest at this point that we separate the person from his behavior, disliking, distrusting, and being angry at rape and incest, for example, rather than at the men who do them. This, they preach, is what "good" women would do.

How can a woman be angry at the "fact" of rape, but not at the rapist? Rape cannot be separated from the rapist, cannot even exist apart from this hate-filled man and his bludgeoning penis (or penis substitute, such as broom handle or knife blade). Since people's actions are the only trustworthy character witnesses for or against them, mountains of behavioral evidence point to the fact that, *as a species,* men are the haters and women the lovers on this planet. Calling women "man-haters," therefore, is classic patriarchal reversal: it is not women who hate men; it is men who hate women.

Patriarchal reversal, one of the most common of men's strategies for obscuring the truth of what is actually happening and who is doing what to whom, even as a term reveals exactly what men are. As mutations of us, they are the reverse, the exact opposite, of all that is female. Since femaleness is truth, maleness operates not only outside the realm of truth, but also in its reverse.

Therefore, turning men's every false "truth" upside down, as Mary Daly suggests, is as close as we can come to a fool-proof method of determining *the* truth. We are not likely to go wrong by believing the opposite of what men tell us is true about almost everything, and virtually can never go wrong by believing the opposite of what their system propounds as true about gender.

"Creating their own reality," as the Toxic Age Movement encourages them to do, is for men basically just more patriarchal reversal, exonerating them and their system while blaming women for all inescapable conditions that in patriarchy pertain to females only. They tell us that, if we experience acts of male violence and treachery in our lives, we have no one to blame but ourselves. Being the creators of our own reality, the "truth," they assure us, is that we have brought these upon ourselves, and that it is totally up to us to bring a different future reality into our lives.

But women have an irresolvable problem here. Though we can seek professional help for trauma caused by men's abuse, and given enough time can grow scar tissue over our emotional wounds, there is absolutely nothing we can do change the reality of gender in patriarchy. We cannot "*un-create* our own reality" of oppression as women because we did not "create" it in the first place. Instead, it was Number One on men's initial "to do" list, and has maintained that position of first priority ever since.

Over a long life, my mind has absorbed countless details of women's suffering at men's hands. These enrage me, break my heart, and in the past have galvanized every cell in my body, every ounce of my strength, to try to stop them.

Though I have to manage it and not let it take over my life, my anger does not alarm me; in fact, I am reassured of my emotional health when I feel it at appropriate times. If I were ever able to contemplate men's relentless viciousness without being moved to anger, that's when I would be alarmed about myself. Such heartlessness masquerading as "objectivity" (emotional coldness being one of men's prime values and characteristics) would not, as men constantly insist, attest to my being better adjusted than women who respond angrily, but quite the opposite. It would mark me as being pathologically unable to empathize, to care, to love. Like men.

Women's anger upsets men more than any other of our emotions. Every man in the world knows full well what men *as a species* think and feel about women and exactly what they do to us. Knowing this, he also knows exactly how justified, infinite, and perhaps non-survivable women's legitimate anger would be if it were loosed upon him. Knowing the retaliation they deserve, masters always fear the anger of the slaves.

So, not surprisingly, men have made women afraid of our anger, too, over the duration of patriarchy punishing us savagely for any evidence of it. Indeed, men's system has become so laden with injunctions and proscriptions against women's anger that most women are veritable walking Vesuviuses of rumbling, roiling, repressed rage. Under the pressures of guilt and fear, women hardly dare give their fury the slightest recognition or expression.

Believing the lie that denying their anger at men's violence will save them from it, women are also terrified at public avowals and displays of *other* women's anger; they vehemently disassociate themselves from them or try to stop them (by screaming, fainting, and running to the river, for instance). The danger seems to be that if they hear even a smidgeon of the truth, they may be unable to prevent their barely controlled volcanoes of rage from erupting with enough force to blast the universe apart.

The truth is, however, that what is more dangerous than having an explosive epiphany is not allowing ourselves to feel anger when it is the only appropriate response. Dampening our fury and sorrow, we also dampen positive feelings such as serenity and gladness, and make a dull grey monotone of the otherwise colorful and lively mosaic of life. Little by little, repression of true and honest feeling deadens our spirits, turns us into zombies. Feeling our anger toward men may frighten us, but better to feel it and learn to direct its great energy into useful channels than to risk neuropathy of the heart.

Or than to release it as a sort of virulent safety-value upon other women, as men have trained us to do.

For obvious male-serving reasons, Toxic-Age doctrine makes "negativity" the worst possible sin, the cause (instead of the result), of all negative behavior. This lie has worked well; even many women who would not call themselves adherents of the Toxic-Age Movement have accepted this as true and are obsessively, almost pathologically, positive about men, though very negative about those of us who are negative about men.

From this we can conclude that the value of negativity is perverse and paradoxical: it is good for women to be negative about feminists who genuinely care about them and bad to be negative about men who genuinely hate them.

For instance, while even a passing comment about men's perpetual war against women is dangerously negative (because it tells the truth about men), speaking against the war in the Middle East is not negative per se. It and all other wars that are not ostensibly against women are safe for women to bemoan; a generalized dislike of war will not bring the Inquisitors to the door. Even some men are negative about war—if, that is, it is defined narrowly enough to exclude the war against women.

However, though most women seem ignorant of it, central to all wars is the deliberate defilement and destruction of women (biblical wars, as you know, are full of it). Not only is this a highly pleasurable activity for men, but destroying women, the enemy's prized possessions, is an accepted, even an honorable, strategy of war. The fact that war has always provided a righteous justification for the rape, torture, and slaughter of women is one of the strongest incentives for men to go to war—and the one kept most secret from Mom and the womenfolk at home.

But yeasty truth will sometimes bubble up through one of the cracks in men's official version of their history despite all their efforts to contain it, and if it isn't pushed back out of sight quickly enough, can offer glimpses of truly monstrous truth.

Take the My Lai incident during the Vietnam war, for instance, where American soldiers, full of misogyny and blood lust, slaughtered the innocent inhabitants of the village called My Lai. Though they killed old men and boy children as well as girls and women, females were quite definitely their major targets: they could be raped and gang-raped to death, their fetuses could be cut out of their stomachs and beheaded before their dying eyes, they could be forced to watch their other children tortured and killed. Yes, in general, women make war lots more exciting.

The political outrage over My Lai here at home turned into a media drama cleverly scripted to manipulate the public into believing that this atrocity was a rare occurrence in the military and deeply regretted. (That it became public was all that was "deeply regretted.")

But this glimpse merely confirmed what many feminists already knew about men and war: that My Lai was just business as usual, just one of hundreds of thousands of such "events" in

men's long history of war, and that men's obsession with raping and killing women in war is as strong as—or perhaps even
stronger than—their obsession with killing enemy soldiers.

Because the truth in mensworld is so incredibly heinous,
all women need illusions in order simply to survive from day
to day. Not surprisingly, most of our illusions, entire worlds of
them, are about men.

One of our customary ways of preserving these sacred illusions is to refer to men's behavior in passive voice, obscuring
not only their identity but their very existence. We all know
this, but we keep forgetting. When we say, for instance, "in
war women are raped," we gloss over the fact that men do the
raping; being absent from the sentence, they are also absent
from the crime scene. When we use passive voice, we supply
men with easy, ready-made alibis.

Active voice, on the other hand, tells the whole truth by
giving us an agent, a perpetrator: "in war," it says, "soldiers
routinely rape women." Keeping the truth clear to ourselves,
then, requires that we always remember to use active voice,
always catch the criminal red-handed—that is, with women's
blood still dripping from his hands. One instance when we as
feminists often forget to do this is in sentences such as: "the
conference was about violence against women." To be sure not
to give men alibis, we need to say instead, "the conference was
about *men's* violence against women."

We also hide the identity of perpetrators of crimes against
women when we make patriarchy itself the villain, as in, "rape
is necessary for the perpetuation of patriarchy."

Patriarchy is men; it neither exists without them nor acts
except through them. As worldview-become-system, patriarchy has no muscles with which to knock us to the ground, no
feet to kick us, no fists to smash our faces, no teeth to bite off

our nipples, no penises to ram into our vaginas; in short, no physical presence to torture, maim, and dehumanize us.

(This is one of the reasons I prefer the word "mensworld" to "patriarchy." "Mensworld" does not allow us to forget *who* patriarchy is.)

Rape is not a weapon of abstract patriarchy; it is a weapon of the flesh-and-blood patriarchs themselves. Blaming rape on "patriarchy" hides the fact that it is real guys of all races, classes, and cultures who do the actual raping. Real guys like "Charlie," the Anglo head of the university's anthropology department, and "Storm Cloud," the Native American shaman, and "Norm," the Jewish doctor at the women's clinic. Patriarchy is totally dependent upon these guys' doing the necessary and exciting woman-hating work of maintaining male supremacy.

Now when there is scarcely anything positive left to say about men, speaking the truth about them has, of course, become patriarchy's most deadly taboo. But breaking taboos is what we do, we radical lovers of women. Telling the truth despite men's imprimatur against its negativity is still our job as it has been throughout the whole of men's long terrorist regime.

In patriarchy *the* truth is difficult to spot and harder still to hold on to, but it does indeed exist, and nowhere clearer and braver than in Radical Feminist philosophy and ontology. "Radical" because it tells the truth that maleness is the "root" of all misery in the world; not only in regard to people, but also to elephants and dolphins, to chickens and dogs, to every species everywhere. This principal elucidates the nature of patriarchy as no other systematic theory does, helping us detect and reject every male lie at the root of patriarchy and replace it with its opposite female truth.

This chapter cannot hold a millionth part of that truth, but fortunately many thousands of other women have written it in the past and are writing and speaking it still throughout the world. There they are, their books and articles and videos, filling the bookcases in feminists' living spaces and spilling over into their attics and garages, making their homes nuclei of insurrection. Though neither they nor these authors may agree with me about the meaning of Radical Feminism, what we can all embrace is women, loving them above everything, being loyal to them even at the risk of our lives.

But, one might ask, why should we even have to face the truth again now at this late date in men's literally god-awful history? Does it really matter all that much?

Though our telling the truth about men enrages them, ultimately it is as much about us as it is about them. With this act, we acknowledge every woman's suffering at men's hands and stand with her in conscious, whole-souled opposition. Breaking this taboo demonstrates that our love for women is stronger than our fear of men, and ultimately stronger than anything else in our lives. Telling the truth attests to our belief that the truth connects the spirits of all women in unfathomable power.

So, yes, if we love women, telling the truth matters. We cannot even imagine how much it matters, what turbulent, dangerous, frightening times lie ahead for us, times when the difference between life and death is knowing who to trust and why. We are on the fast track to a moment in patriarchal history when either knowing or not knowing what men really are will decide our fate.

Right now, today, we need to look fearlessly at the truth of our Stockholming and wrestle this malignant enemy out of our hearts, this fierce and perverse attachment to men who *as a species* have never wished us anything but harm, who from their beginnings have been our most merciless enemies, and have tricked us endlessly into believing that their bitter hatred of us constitutes "love."

We need to recognize with absolute clarity the truth that when it comes to a choice between their privilege and our lives, they will—and do every day—unhesitatingly choose their privilege. More than this, though, we need to understand, not only with our superficial brains but to the very depths of our souls, how addicted they are to causing us pain on every level of our lives and how they hunger to destroy us.

There is not much time left. If we want to survive, in either flesh or spirit, we need to wake up quickly. We have no more time to enjoy our cozy Toxic-Age slumber or our sweet, romantic idealism. Truth is our torch now, the only guide we have. Though from all sides everything and everybody may be shouting at us to go the male-dictated direction, truth can and will keep us on the opposite female course.

Acknowledging the truth to ourselves because it is our essence, respecting and embracing it no matter how painful, and having the courage to act on it—this is what loving one another looks like now, what loving this planet and every form of beneficent life means.

Choosing the truth now, choosing femaleness over maleness—because it *will*, perhaps already *has*, come to this—means letting go of as many illusions about men as we can: our conditioned beliefs, for instance, that we need them for "balance;" that women and men are the same species, sharing the same nature and destiny; that *any* man exists who can, in the final analysis, be believed and trusted; and, most painful of all to relinquish, the illusion that they, who are the opposites of our loving female selves, have the capacity to love us as we love them.

Finally, our activism is to choose to live, consciously and every minute of every day, in the truth basic to all truth: that femaleness is the only power, the only good, the only happiness in this or any universe, now or ever, and that no matter what else happens, it will prevail and flourish.

The truth that being female is the best of all possible good fortune.

PART IV

Being There

Chapter 10

Home Again

Sitting here at my desk thinking about Monique Wittig—how sure she was that the female world once existed, how fiercely she instructed us to remember and invent it, as if in doing so we might help restore it—I am indescribably moved. I share her love for that world and her conviction that it is real. Eager to help in any way I can, I am about to try an experiment.

So, I prepare. Moving onto the sofa, I breathe deeply and relax, putting the brakes on my rampaging brain. I close my eyes, reach back, back . . .

Time, at once so flexible and so fragile, begins to stretch out thin, weakening.

Remember . . . remember . . .

With my eyes still closed, I feel the warmth of the sun on my face, and the power and grace of female beings touching my heart like a benediction, their presence almost tangible, tingly on my outstretched fingers.

But still I don't open my eyes, content to sit forever in the peace of their presence on this hillside, content to let their auras of well-being heal my time-battered soul. Mindless, at rest, I listen to the colloquy of trees and grass in the wind and the distant sound of the sea; these susurruses—as well as a sound I can't identify—almost resound against a background of profoundest silence.

The quality of this silence informs me that I have for this moment escaped the prison of time again and am—at least to some degree—once again in the timeless female world, the world as it was before the advent of maleness. I am surprised at having been able to be here at will.

But I'm afraid that if I move too quickly, or open my eyes too soon, I'll awaken from the dream and plunge back into men's nightmare. So to hold on to this tenuous awareness, I keep my eyes closed.

Ah. The sound I couldn't recognize at first now seems to me to be a sort of music . . . so unlike any music I have known and loved in mensworld that my linear ears can hardly make sense of it. It seems fuller somehow, richer, as if each voice is singing several parts at once—no, as if there are no parts or separate notes but all the notes together, all at once; as if the music is round and I'm not able to negotiate the curves quickly enough. Though I'm sure I'm not hearing it fully, the sound is still so sensually strong and sweet as to be almost unbearable. Calling it "music" diminishes it, but there is no other word.

Unlike men's music, this seems to be rising spontaneously out of the essence of all living beings, the resonance of female life everywhere. Spontaneous, playful and passionate, it spills down the air and sifts through the leaves of the trees. I realize that even I, here only in memory and imagination, only a visitor, am not just listening but am somehow involved in its creation—though I am not aware of doing anything. I conclude that simply being alive where all is female is to be literally harmonious, generating audible, visceral joy, cadences of well-being delicious to every sense.

I call to mind my most loved passages of patriarchal music, and realize that unlike them, this in which I am participating so effortlessly is free from the falseness of deliberate composition and performance. It is the sound of clouds and birds savoring their lives, of life delighting itself in all of us. I am charmed that we are making this multidimensional, harmonically exquisite music simply by existing; that this music is us—us loving ourselves and one another.

Not only hearing it with my ears but also in my skin and hair and along every nerve, I become aware of faint responses in my body, many forgotten senses awakening that have lain dormant so long in mensworld that they hardly remember what they're about. I'm excited by beginning to experience this sound in so many forgotten ways.

Even the air feels female here, redolent of rain and flowers, clean and tender on my face. I can smell the salt of the sea, and the loamy muskiness of fertile soil and vegetation as it drifts around me in the sunshine. But even as I feel almost faint with fragrance, I know that everywhere here there are odors my nose still cannot remember how to register, odors it can't distinguish from colors and sounds and feelings.

Probably in this female world these senses are not separate but, together, endlessly find new ways to experience and interpret color and form, odor and texture. Femaleness is creativity. Nothing about it is static, every living thing part of a pulsing ocean of energy and power.

Sometime in the last few moments I have opened my eyes and now, like the fulfillment of a promise, my planet lies before me, radiant with health, glorious beyond description, the trees and grass burning with the green of free, unthreatened life. As I look down from my perch past the treetops and out at the distant sea, I am perfectly at peace.

Though at first I see no sign of the female beings in whose midst I sit, I nevertheless feel their presence. Then, here and there, I see light shimmering in the air, and memories stir in my mind: the first males unable to see the female beings women once were, our bodies composed of such exquisitely fine matter that we were transparent to them; females changing our shape and substance so to be seen and to communicate.

Now I, with my crude human eyes, like those first men, see them only as reflected sunlight.

Still, though I can't see them, everything about them feels familiar to me; in a global way, I know them, though I can offer no description except to say that their effect is to fill me with happiness. This is femaleness, I marvel; this is me, my Self. These beings know me, too—not in the general way I know them but as my particular female Self; and, knowing this, know me far better than I know myself. Unfortunately, it is not hard for free, non-conditioned females to know any conquered woman better than she knows herself.

Relaxed and happy knowing they are there, I lie back in the air ... *in the air?* ... above a lake of flowers that ripples in the breeze, gently brushing my back and legs. Their colors surprise me, so many I've never seen before or could even have imagined. I quickly give up trying to think of names for them (why do I think I have to name them?), these perky little blossoms by my left knee, for instance, that couldn't be more fragrant. Or taste more luminous.

Just as I suspected: my unruly senses seem to have forgotten their patriarchically-assigned jobs. Because they are rushing about in wild arousal, bumping into, falling over and merging into one another, I'm unsure whether I'm seeing or smelling or tasting a color. Or feeling it. Each flower's form and pigment—its essence—exerts its own visceral effect upon me. Color by color, vibration upon vibration—cool, tangy, iridescent to my tongue, my fingertips, my eyes, my nose—I become first one then the other, then all of them together. I am part of this sensory celebration, a flower among flowers, my delicate body now a melting of petal into caress into iridescence into perfume.

This is intimacy, women's home; for these few moments I am home again. I close my eyes, and imagine other moments of deep connection that await me here, not only with my own species, but with females of every kind: my spider's legs against the silken undersides of these petals, my bird's wings lifted by the waves of airy sea overhead, my immense whale body in the weightless embrace of ocean, my insect feelers stroking bark, stalks, blades. Me, being the planet and all living beings touching and energizing one another, touching and adoring one another. And at the same time being my own woman-self, adoring, touching, being all women.

I am that bear and that unicorn wandering together into the woods, walking so lightly their feet don't seem to be touching the ground . . . unicorn? Good heavens, it's a unicorn!

(I do not stop now to wonder why I wander from female consciousness back to male, but realize at the end of this amazing day that I am unable to sustain an infinite, timeless female reality very thoroughly or for long, but that I can't help superimposing men's small, time-and-brain-bound paradigm upon most of it.)

Now as I watch the bear and the unicorn melt into the forest, a little brown girl—still such a baby that she shouldn't even be able to walk and certainly shouldn't be out here alone—steps confidently out of the trees. She begins to climb the hill toward me, her feet a few inches off the ground. Looking up directly into my eyes, she greets me with such a happy smile that I'm sure she has mistaken me for someone else.

Then, just as I rise to meet her, a panther springs into her path. Wildly, I look around for the baby's mother—surely she's here somewhere! But no one seems to be watching this child, so despite my crashing heart, I dash down the hill to her rescue . . .

And am instantly the little girl, seeing through her eyes, experiencing her feelings as if they were my own, while also being my own astonished self. Now, with her eyes, I really see the panther, fiery black in the sun, throbbing with energy, her whole being radiating gladness. And, like the little girl, I am so happy to meet her that I laugh aloud as we fling our arms around her neck.

Tumbling down, we roll about with one another several inches above the ground, our arms and legs entwined, kissing and licking, laughing and growling, tickling and stroking, each feeling not only what we ourselves feel but simultaneously feeling exactly what the others are feeling. From the moment I begin experiencing being all three of us at once, I hardly know which of us is me.

Or care.

Gradually, the scuffle subsides and we hold one another quietly, suspended in the air, still breathless, relishing our closeness. Then the child springs lightly onto the panther's back, and away they glide toward the trees.

On the fringes of the forest, they stop and look back at me and I raise my hand—not in farewell, but in acknowledgement that the our amazing connection will never diminish. Since entropy of any variety—physical or spiritual—is impossible without time, in the timeless female universe intimacy is everlasting.

As they slip away into the forest, their pleasure in our friendship reaches across the distance and clasps my upraised hand, their affection brushes my face. Even after they disappear, I stand looking after them for a moment, reluctant to let them go.

But I am full of questions that interrupt this mood. What is going on with the little girl? Why hasn't someone come looking for her? Why doesn't anyone seem worried?

Where on earth is her *mother?*

❧ ❧ ❧

Chapter 11

Parthenogenesis, Babies, and Motherhood

I am unaware until she touches my arm that, seemingly out of nowhere, a human-like woman has alighted next to me. I know that, for my sake, she has taken this shape and become visible. Naked, she appears ageless, and like everything here, is surrounded by a shimmering halo of golden energy. Looking directly into my eyes with great intelligence and kindness, she smiles and takes my hand.

"There is no such thing as 'mother' here," she tells me without words. "Try to remember . . . ."

I lie back down above the flowers, and contemplate the fact of this particular child, this panther-riding, walking-on-air baby. As I do, I realize immediately what a great deal of conditioning I am going to have to override, so I begin by asking myself the easy question:

How did my young friend come physically into the world?

Parthenogenetically, of course. I don't have to think long about the answer to this; feminists have been theorizing about parthenogenesis for years and lately seem to be even more interested than usual.

Certainly, women are still, today, giving birth parthenogenetically. There is no more doubt of this than that there are women who still fly, those who breathe under water, those who become invisible, those who walk through walls. On occasion, most women momentarily slip back into our female way of being and unwittingly do the "impossible." Afterwards, unable to believe our own senses, we explain it away: "I must have forgotten opening the door and walking through it into this room."

Many more women have reproduced parthenogenetically in this world during patriarchy and up to this moment than we will ever know—or that often they themselves will ever know. If a woman was married or having sex with a man during the time she became pregnant, she naturally assumed that conception took place in the conventional patriarchal way. That her daughter may be her sole genetic responsibility will very likely never occur to her.

But enough women have been sure they could not have conceived in the conventional manner—and have proved it medically—that we are left in no doubt. Perhaps some of these women knew what they were doing when they conceived , but I suspect most of them simply, out of habit, did automatically what they had done so easily for all the eternities they had lived without males.

Originally, before maleness struck, menstruation may not have been part of reproduction at all. Since we could begin the process at will, our wombs would not have needed a fertility cycle. Only after the advent of men and time, when men began raping and sexually enslaving us, would we have needed to develop one. Menstruation is women's adaptation to male ownership and relentless desecration of our bodies.

Before men, women—consciously, knowledgeably—were our entire bodies at once, perfect harmony and complete connection and understanding from head to foot, not separate but each part also every other part as well as the whole. Therefore, deciding to have a child was not solely the brain's decision; every atom of all organs was involved. Our uterus readied herself, the ovum did her thing, the cells became their new selves, the entire body went into creating mode—all at once.

In addition, none of this phenomenon needed to be regulated from central headquarters—the moon, or anything else. Our bodies were independently creative, capable of anything at any time. And certainly not on a linear time line any more than moons and tides were.

Though we were in complete harmony with the moon and all planets and stars, and were so profoundly connected to them that we *were* them, we were free beyond the word's ultimate meaning in any language. None of us controlled any other, even gently. If we influenced the moon, it was because we were her; if she influenced us, it was by being us.

Being is not understandable by the patriarchal mind; maleness is incapable of being, can only *try* to be, and "trying to be" is an oxymoron: trying is doing. All of us, unfortunately, are stranded now in that doing mode; a large part of becoming pregnant parthenogenetically, then, is *not* to think about it, *not* to try.

Parthenogenesis, describing reproduction in all females of every species and kind, remains such a radical, such a heretical, dangerous departure from male dicta, that it calls into question every hallowed belief on the subject of reproduction. Especially men's belief (or desperate hope) that they play an essential part in it.

How did males even enter the picture in the first place?

The most common non-conformist theory (assuming that the two most conformist are creationism and evolution) is that maleness is a result of internal damage to female chromosomes from the Big Bang; that it was after that explosion that the human race, the mortals, made their first appearance on the universe's stage.

Before their arrival, globally, universally, the female population was very small. If we gave birth at all, we were certainly not the frenzied breeders we subsequently became under men's domination and for their purposes. All species knew instinctively the right number of offspring necessary to maintain perfect balance on the planet, and produced only that number.

One thing is certain: every conception was a totally free choice, such as conception can never be in patriarchy. Women today will argue heatedly about this, insisting that they do make totally free choices to have babies, uninfluenced by anything or anyone else. Perhaps this is possible, but most likely it is just one illusion among the hundreds, maybe thousands, we carry around with us in mensworld. We have no way of knowing our true motives in this paradigm.

Males emerged universally in nearly every species, weak (and therefore violent), vulnerable, sex-crazed, and so terrified of extinction that after they found they could do it, they fucked and begat desperately, frenetically, disastrously. The world began to fill with babies, and the human race (that by this time females had entered by adaptation) was among the top producers. But these babies were, and are, very different creatures from parthenogenetic babies.

Since all babies in patriarchy, female as well as male, are helpless at birth, the conventional belief today is that helplessness is the true nature of babies, the way they have always been and will always be. Though certainly some babies develop more quickly than others, none of them at six months, even at a year—even at three years—comes close to panther-baby's physical and emotional independence.

Baby girls in the female universe, though we were small, were complete females among females, total power from birth, having lost nothing simply by exchanging our former bodies for new ones. Knowing everything, we had nothing to learn; the idea of "learning" would not even exist in a world where everyone *is* all there is to know, an infinity of knowledge.

Life in the female world was not a school. It was not about studying to become wiser, or trying to become stronger or healthier, or accomplishing things, or overcoming difficulties, or learning from experience. Every female being was completely wise, strong, healthy, and knowledgeable—perfect—just as she was.

Femaleness was about being, and solely about being, a concept almost impossible to grasp in mensworld where all is about doing—learning, achieving, becoming.

As female children before patriarchy, so innately full of power and intelligence, we needed nothing but the never-failing, eternally abundant love that permeated us and filled the world around us. Peers with everyone, and small dynamos of energy production, we needed no one to be responsible for us. "Responsible" was unthinkable. Not only were we not helpless, but we were unlimited power, totally known, universally respected and adored, in a world where "hurt" and "harm" were neither imaginable nor possible.

I understand now why neither panther-baby's mother nor some designated caretaker rushed to save her when the big cat swung into her path. That powerful little child *had* no "mother" in the terms men have brainwashed us to believe is necessary. And no need for one.

Motherhood first came into the world with maleness, the use of women as an energy source necessary for the survival of male children, who were born and remained powerless and dependent upon female energy all their lives. Motherhood is a basic institution of patriarchy, absolutely essential for the survival of men. No such role, no role at all for any purpose, was either possible or necessary prior to their existence.

In the female paradigm, where "use" of anything, ever, was not a possibility, giving birth did not instantly make her a "usable" object, did not saddle her with a lifetime role as caregiver and resource. In fact, in the female world we were as free of roles as in mensworld we are almost nothing *but* roles. Mother, daughter, sister, grandmother, aunt, lover, wife—all are female functions that sustain men, roles that designate ways in which female energy is usurped to anchor and sustain families, patriarchy's superstructure.

Now as patriarchy weakens and fear fills the earth, not the conservatives alone but nearly the entire population seems desperate to remind us that the family is the bedrock of society and must at all costs be preserved.

Of course, when anyone says "society" they refer to patriarchy, the planet's only organized belief system. The family, the most egregious theft of female power on earth, is the very foundation of male survival and therefore of patriarchy.

Because of this, lovers of women and of freedom grant the family no respect, to say nothing of veneration. In fact, we are pleased that the family as a male construct will disappear along with all other maleness and that no amount of preaching and admonishing can save it. It has always been riddled with the weakness of sadomasochism, but now, right before our eyes, we watch it in the last stages of rot.

Imagine a world with no families, none of the terrible experiences women have in them: imagine no belief that women's entire purpose is to be used, physically, emotionally, spiritually, intellectually. Imagine no marital rape, no incest, no subordination, no emotional or physical violence, no financial or emotional dependency, no unwanted motherhood, no roles, no coercion, no slavery.

Imagine a world where giving birth does not sell any woman into energy-source slavery for the rest of her life, nor designate her as worthy only because she can now be used— and used up—by others. Where neither she nor anyone else thinks of any child as "hers," since giving birth does not bestow ownership—a concept totally antithetical to femaleness.

Imagine a world in which having given birth entails no fatigue, no resentment, no worry or guilt or feelings of failure in the present or down the line.

And no post-partum blues. Though such depression is partially hormonal, it is also partly the unconscious knowledge that the ubiquitous propaganda extolling motherhood has trapped us. Having fallen for it, there is now no honorable way out so that, whether we want to or not, we must make ourselves and all our energy and resources available at all times. We are depressed at the vision of the future now looming before us of having to take care of this person in one way or another for the rest of our lives. We are beginning to see already how unlikely we are to be able to fulfill the unrealistic expectations that are part and parcel of motherhood. And now that it is too late, we're not even sure we want to try.

But to be conscious of these feelings would be unbearable, so, perhaps out of guilt, or hopelessness, or some other less than healthful motive, we have another baby, and another. And bit by bit lose track of our real feelings—lose ourselves.

Imagine a world in which women do not have to take care of children (or anything or anyone else), where no one needs to be taken care of, where caretaking is not even possible.

Then imagine a child who never sees a face that is cross, or tired, or impatient, or bruised, or tear-streaked. Who sees instead only the faces of women, animals, insects, fishes, and birds that reflect the pure desire to cuddle her, nuzzle her, stroke her, lick her, play with her; where every living thing in her ken is totally thrilled with her.

Imagine the self-esteem of a child who, because no one is ever forced to care for her, brings nothing but obvious delight to everyone.

Imagine a world in which we are not conditioned to believe we need to have a baby of our own, that we should even desire one, or that procreation is the supreme reason for our being. Imagine touching and being touched in such thoroughly satisfying physical and spiritual ways all the time that we do not need babies—as many women need them now—in order to have someone to hold and caress and kiss who does not make us pay for it with sex.

Imagine a world in which childbearing is pure, never entered into for anyone's approval or for pseudo-prestige or to feel like a real woman, a useful woman, a righteous, obedient woman, a woman whose life is given meaning by service.

Imagine a world where knowing we are immortal, we feel no compulsion to seek eternal life, as men do in vain, through our posterity. Imagine a world where we have a baby for no other reason than to bring more joy into our midst.

What is certain is that all this disappeared and we began to change radically—physically and emotionally—the instant males struck the universe, bearing within themselves the seeds of their own destruction, and posing infinite danger to the female universe.

Chapter 12

Reconsidering Chapter 11

The inexplicability of timelessness to our time-bound minds makes the whole issue of reproduction almost impossible to consider. But it is just one of the multitude of ways we and our world were not only profoundly different, but antithetical to men and to their world in which we are now stranded.

The greatest danger in any attempt to imagine a profoundly alien paradigm is that we will be too conservative; that faced with the discomfort of the incomprehensible, we will unconsciously impose upon it our familiar and cozy patriarchal assumptions and worldview.`

Rereading the last chapter, I see that I have done just that. From what mis-memory or erring invention did the little girl come?

From a series of unconscious assumptions.

We look at ourselves, our breasts, our vaginas, our wombs, and we say, "We are mammals."

But were we always?

In a timeless world, how could we have been? Timeless means ageless, non-linear, all-at-once. In such a world we could not have begun as embryos, developed along a time-line to fetuses, growing bigger, more complex until ready for birth. Such a process, like all processes, is linear. Dependent upon linear time, gestation, therefore, would have been impossible.

In fact, the problem of process raises questions about any attribute we bestow on the timeless female universe, a universe where nothing becomes but always simply is. Process is about movement through time, and is therefore antithetical to the female paradigm; when we resort to it in any explanation of femaleness, we are instantly in a misogynist universe.

Though this fact should make all speculation about femaleness useless—since we truly cannot think out of time and process—every now and then, as we bumble about trying to remember and invent our original, much-missed selves, our spirits slip for a moment out of patriarchy into a place of unutterable loveliness. This is reason enough to go on.

So, going on.

In a timeless world, without entropy, degeneration, or corruptibility, aging and death would have been as nonparadigmatic as conception and birth. Also, in that world body and spirit would have been indivisible, integral entities incapable of separation. Since separation is one of the hallmarks of maleness—as unity is of femaleness—death is entirely male.

This means there was no birth in the female world, no babies, no motherhood, no death. Uncreated, always existing, females had no beginning and no end.

If we assume for the moment that in our original world we did not conceive—parthenogenetically or in any other way— we would have needed no vaginas, no wombs, no breasts, no ovaries. Perhaps we were clitoral from head to foot, one large sensory pleasure-and-joy-producing organism, all-powerful, all-loving, all-connected with every other living thing.

I know that many women would be dismayed at the thought of a world in which there were no children; most women love children, and for this and many other reasons want babies. For many women, children are one of the few sources of happiness in mensworld—at least, this is what we are taught to believe by men's propaganda: TV, movies, songs, books, educational and religious institutions of both the left and right political persuasions.

But I remember that about 25 years ago, someone wrote to Ann Landers and suggested asking parents this question: if you could do your life over again knowing what you know now, would you have children?

That poll generated over 10,000 replies, 96 per cent of which said, essentially, "not a chance!" (Over the intervening quarter of a century, I have come across several similar studies with similar findings, the most recent in the July 7/July 14, 2008, issue of Newsweek: "Having Kids Makes You Happy.")

This is not to prove that women do not really love children; women are the lovers of the universe. Nor is it an attempt to prove that they do not want them. It simply suggests that our reasons for having them are deeply opaque to us. Implanted by the media, or by spousal or other family or religious pressures, the reasons almost always originated from men's relentless programming: that bearing their offspring is the most noble, the most "feminine," the most desirable of all female goals and behavior, and the one that will make us most fulfilled and happy. And often the one that will persuade men that we are too valuable to kill.

What it comes down to is that we have babies for such a multitude of reasons unrelated to the children themselves or to the actual role of motherhood that to see our true motives in this matter now would be nothing short of miraculous.

As I have thought about this, I have always ended up back at this premise: before the Big Bang and the introduction of time/maleness into the universe, we could have been neither mammalian nor human. But in playing devil's advocate with myself, I argued:

Assuming conception and birth for a moment, why would the bionic panther-riding baby, so innately full of power and intelligence, able always to be instantly wherever and whatever she wished to be—why would she have needed to develop inside another female's body?

A characteristic that most distinguishes femaleness and separates it as a species from maleness is its non-consumption—its non-use—of the energy of any other living thing. Unlike maleness—for which the first question always is: "How can I use it? What is it good for? How can it benefit me"?—femaleness does not pirate energy, is not parasitical in essence, does not use or consume. It could therefore be argued that parthenogenesis—or any other form of reproduction—that uses female bodies and consumes female energy, could not have been the norm in the pre-patriarchal, exclusively-female world.

However, in an effort to make reproduction somehow fit the assumptions of our patriarchal minds, we might speculate that, rather than using another female's body, in the female paradigm each individual would have been more likely to have created her own body out of her own energy and with her own power.

But creation implies beginnings, and beginnings are relevant only in time. Since the female universe was timeless and everyone always existed, there was no need for anyone to "create" themselves or anyone else. To "create" is to "do," and "doing" requires linear time.

The only way reproduction would have been reasonable in that world is if we were a species that periodically needed to replace our used bodies with fresh ones. But, being timeless, we were not such a species; entropy is the great de-generator, and entropy is inherent in time, nonexistent outside it. Our non-human/non-mammalian bodies, therefore, composed of highly refined, perhaps nearly translucent, and blindingly powerful immortal matter, could never wear out, never grow "old," never need replacing.

Nor would we have needed death to regenerate our weary spirits. Like our bodies, our spirits were non-ravaged by time and entropy, and by all conditions and circumstances that cause deterioration of physical and spiritual well-being in mensworld. Since no living thing was subject to the linearity of male/time cause-and-effect, in the female universe there were no ills that either flesh or spirit were heir to.

In addition, since all life was female, no other beings used any of our energy, let alone gorged on it as males of every species have done increasingly from their beginnings up to this time. Even we ourselves did not "use" one another's energy; we had no need to. Quite the opposite, in fact: each of us was a champion life-energy generator. The power we were, the infinite and everlasting energy we each were, filled the universe.

Not until after the Big Bang brought maleness, time, and mammalia into possibility in the universe (and in us, since we were the universe) did our physical devolution reach the point where our veins flowed with blood—a highly corruptible mammalian substance. If indeed we even had a circulatory system before the advent of maleness, the fluid in them would have been like *ichor*, the incorruptible "blood" of the Greek immortals. (We have a good idea where *that* idea came from!)

We need only ask ourselves, does god have body-replacement issues? Does god's spirit falter and need refreshing?

No study of the females of any species—no matter how "in-depth"—can reveal today what we really are, only what maleness has forced us to be. Without doubt, all female beings universe-wide—animals, birds, plants, reptiles, fish, insects (maybe even mountains, oceans, air)—were altogether *other* than anything we can imagine now. And men have deliberately erased all knowledge of this amazing world, of this amazing *us*, from the hard-disk of universal consciousness.

But those of us who were those amazing beings sometimes experience, seemingly for no reason, flashes of intense well-being, a welling up of great power within ourselves. Then, for a few blessed seconds, we remember that we are, in our essence, still a stupendously powerful species of beings.

How did all this change? How did maleness invade Eden?

Some theorists hypothesize that the stunted male y is a result of damage to the original X chromosome in a fertilized egg, probably caused by the force and/or radioactivity of the Big Bang. If this had been the case, women would have had to have been either created or to have evolved—both of which can occur only in time.

So we have a choice: we can believe men—the creationists or the evolutionists—or we can believe women of very ancient cultures who assure us that, before the advent of maleness, females lived forever in a male-less, timeless world.

If we choose to believe women—and credit our own memories and intuition—that females are immortal, without beginning or end, whereas males are a very recent 180-degrees-twisted mutant branch of our tree, the question of how the Big Bang brought maleness into existence becomes very puzzling indeed.

One possibility is that, since the material of which females were originally composed—and that carried our life story in every cell (if indeed we were composed of cells)—was not exclusively physical, the havoc wreaked by the Big Bang need not have taken place *inside* our bodies. The tremendous energy of our indestructible life-force, of every atom of our amazing bodies—however they were organized, however they appeared—and of our loving souls: this nimbus of life and power swirled endlessly around and through our bodies, perfusing us and all life everywhere—*from* all of us *to* all of us.

The mutilation that introduced the mutation of maleness into our world could very well have occurred in that glowing cloud of possibility. If the enormous *contra*-thrust (reversal of female power) of the Big Bang were introduced into this metapowerful aura, it is possible to imagine a resultant twisting force through which—rather than through a physical birth canal—maleness could have found entrance into physical being—thus created not by a supreme being but by a fateful twist of energy. (or as Jade only half-jokingly suggests, perhaps the first man appeared as a malignant growth on a woman's rib—if we had ribs.)

This fits with Jesse Raven Tree's teaching that men are women's opposites: Since women are non-created and immortal, men therefore are created and mortal.

Though what happened is far from certain, what is certain is that when maleness finally arrived on the scene, it carried within it some female energy—later to become the X chromosome—and its own fatal little y.

Also certain is that included in its disastrous genetic baggage were all its mutant characteristics, the three most significant being the inability to adapt or connect; the sadomasochistic obsession with destruction, even—or particularly—of its own environmental support system (all of which is female); and, as a species, its short life-span.

Before maleness/time, before mammalia, the energy we were was unlimited and powerful beyond any vision of men's gods. Female energy—the only energy that exists, that has ever existed, that will ever exist—is the basis of everything, of all that is intangible and ineffable as well as of all matter. This is a given of our essence and our paradigm.

The consequence of the Big Bang's interference with and interruption of this power in immortal women was the mortal race of men. And subsequently, the physical devolution of women.

When time brought mammalia with it into the universe, females could no longer maintain ourselves as the beings we genuinely were. Just as time and maleness are synonymous, so are femaleness and timelessness. With the explosion, time/maleness began to press down heavily upon us, slowly, perhaps over millennia, forcing limiting, coarsening change upon our bodies and minds.

Finally, adapting to survive maleness and time, we devolved into mammals. Still being powerful and almost infinitely adaptable we may not have needed eons to make this change. Becoming ever more deeply subject to time and to birth and death, we began to reproduce ourselves parthenogenetically.

The question, of course, is not whether parthenogenesis occurred in "humans"—because of course it did and still does—but when it began to occur.

Parthenogenesis may have been an adaptive step out of the female world on our heartbreaking path down into patriarchy's "womanhood." It may have been a space or middle ground—a compromise, if you will—between no use of women's bodies or energy and the total use of them ultimately made by men; an attempt to preserve a last vital freedom before our total assimilation into mensworld. As such, it would have been successful for awhile, allowing us at least briefly to retain some reproductive autonomy.

Somewhere toward the end of our journey out of our Selves into mammalia (of a sort), we became physically rapable, and so, of course, men began to rape us, rape quickly becoming the bridge of choice for maleness to cross into physical bodies.

From their beginnings, men raped us continually, first of our life energy, then in addition, and even more disastrously, of our physical integrity. Raped us until we were so broken, so thoroughly "seasoned" to be sex slaves, that our degraded bodies forgot how to reproduce themselves parthenogenetically.

Though women the world over are still capable of parthenogenesis, our continued inability to reproduce ourselves consciously is a function of our terrorized minds and wills, an artifact of our global sexual slavery. The heartening fact, however, is that unconsciously women, at times, still do reproduce in this way.

ୡ୰ ୡ୰ ୡ୰

Although we became mammalian, we became a very different sort of mammal from the human variety, to this day retaining power far beyond human capacity or understanding, intact, waiting . . . .

We have never lost our original essence, or our capacity to return to our former selves when time and maleness walk together off life's stage. Though we appear to be human and mortal, and despite the untold damage we have suffered at men's hands, we are still the beings who *fly*!

Here's to us, that we fly again soon!

ୡ୰ ୡ୰ ୡ୰

Chapter 13

New Friends

While I have been thinking about conception, babies, and motherhood, the afternoon has quietly slipped away. Now as a huge red sun sinks into a fiery sea, other women join us—my new friend of the morning still at my side. Some come laughing and romping toward us just above the flowers with their large animal friends—elephants, horses, lions—at their sides; others, in clouds of birds and butterflies, drift down through the treetops; and still others—with small furry animals nestled in the curves of their necks and elbows and riding on their heads—simply appear, then sit or recline in the air near us.

All being in shapes I recognize and visible just for me, I know.

When we have assembled, as if at some unspoken cue we rise as one and sail up through the faint stars just now appearing in the sky. High above the darkening sea, on billows of cooling air, we arrange ourselves in a deep circle with our arms around one another; hands clasping paws, snakes twining arms and necks; soft fur warming cool naked shoulders; hips and stomachs settling comfortably against other hips and stomachs; manes and tails and hair caressing backs, cheeks, and necks; spider feet deliciously tickling fur and skin, feathers and scales.

Women and animals of every variety, every size and color, birds, reptiles, fish, insects—laughing, stroking, nibbling, climbing across one another, as if unable to get enough of being together. Gradually, however, a quiet contentment comes over us.

Then, from the earth below and from the surrounding skies, from us and all living things, evening songs flow out upon the dusk. Crescendo, diminuendo—the music of our spontaneous compositions rises and falls as if we are one vast instrument, all our voices weaving in and out in an intricacy of intelligence, passion, and grace. With seemingly infinite varieties of tonality and style, strong and free, everyone's song somehow blends with all others in perfect harmony.

This music—if the female world were only this music, it would be enough.

As it fades to a lovely background pianissimo, the women communicate with one another, and from planet to planet across the universe, in ways and on levels that are incomprehensible to me, though I do recognize quiet laughter. Since I can't understand, I begin to doze, curled up against a dolphin who pats me absently and goes on "talking" with her Cassiopeian friend.

And I dream—or is it a dream?—that I hear a horse whinnying in the distance, and a very soft clop clop of hooves. Wide awake at once, I leap up and dash out of the crowd to watch for her, and am delighted to see her trotting down to me through the moonlight. As she slows to a stop, she whinnies, and I laugh with pleasure: she has invited me for a ride.

Grabbing a handful of mane, I leap weightlessly onto her back and off we go, galloping high over dark mountains and plains, over starlit seas, her great equine muscles contracting and stretching, contracting and stretching as she flies full out now above rainforests where hundreds of waterfalls, ghostly with starlight, tumble down into invisible rivers. Tropical storms crash and shriek around us. Exhilarated by their ferocity, we gallop madly through the night.

With dawn not far off, we pass over Africa and at my un-spoken request land on Mt. Mlanje. I look across the great dark valley to the east and once again see the fires burning on Soche Hill. A sorrow from another life awakens painfully and I let the tears run unchecked off my chin.

And then, instantly, I am back on the familiar flower-flooded hillside above the sea. I slide off the back of my horse friend who in parting nuzzles my face with her big, soft, sweet-smelling lips and—disappears. Women—naked as they always appear to me—brush my shoulders and arms with their lips and fingertips, murmuring melodically as they pass in the early morning mist, the sweet strong music of their lives floating behind them. My shining new friend separates her-self from them and comes to my side. She embraces me and, singing softly, strokes my hair, wipes my tear-streaked face.

She knows without my saying that I am feeling the sharp contrast between the intimacy I have experienced in my short visit here and what passes for intimacy in the world of men to which I must return. She sits quietly while I am ambushed by unwelcome memories: the humiliation and disappointment of trying to find intimacy with men who think it is synonymous with fucking; the grief of discovering that intimacy does not automatically come with caring deeply about women; my life-long ache for a closeness that is not possible in mensworld.

While I pour out this misery, she suffuses me with comfort from her rich center, and assures me wordlessly, but with great clarity, that relief for women's wounded and exhausted spirits in patriarchy is even now on its way.

ᘉᕽᘉ   ᘉᕽᘉ   ᘉᕽᘉ

Chapter 14

Intimacy, the SisterWitch Essence

As a child and young adult, I was homesick for something for which I had no words. Searching for it constantly, I read mountains of books, played and listened to years of music, sat through innumerable classes, found and lost the only woman friend that really mattered, got married and had children, earned meaningless degrees, taught at universities, lived in foreign countries. Always on the lookout.

But all I really managed to do in 41 years of searching was to distract myself from longing for it—whatever it was. Then in the mid-1970's I ran head on into the Women's Movement.

And then! Oh my . . . then!

The vision of women rising out of slavery together all over the world split my life wide open. I rejoiced in our insurgent sisterhood, our fierce, woman-loving global community. I understood deeply that I had more in common with any woman in the world than I had with any man no matter how liberal he was, no matter how alternative. My heart was full to bursting with the dream of women's world—the community of intimates. I was ready to give my life for it.

But as years went by, I realized with sadness that the dream could never come true in patriarchy. The word "patriarchy" says it all: the rule of the fathers, male supremacy, hierarchy. Since equality is the bedrock of intimacy, there can be no genuine intimacy, no possibility of literal oneness, when the fact that half the people of the world rules the other half makes hierarchy the basis of reality.

When I was a young woman—and I believe it is still true—intimacy primarily meant sex. "They've been intimate, you know," meant they had had sex. But after every experience of intercourse in my 20-year marriage, even though it usually ended in orgasm, I felt almost no spiritual connection with my husband and certainly no intimacy. I knew I would recognize intimacy if I ever felt it, and I feared that if I didn't find it in sex, I would never find it.

Anyway, that was the warning from men, the authors of my socialization.

I had no language, no word but "intimacy," for what I knew I was capable of feeling, and "intimacy" as it was commonly used fell far short of what I had in mind.

By the time I became a feminist one night in a mormon church meeting—not just a feminist but an incipient radical feminist ("radical" in the sense of "roots," my having been catapulted that night into the clear knowledge that men were the roots of patriarchy)—I already admired women, and soon learned to love them, but for another six years didn't think I needed to have sex with them—actually didn't feel like having sex with them. My lesbian friends insisted, however, that sex with women was different, that to be a Lesbian and to be intimate with women was the same thing.

The "intimate" part persuaded me. So I tried it, and discovered that my friends had been right about one thing at least—sex was more pleasant with women.

But it was not what I was searching for. Sex with women was still sex, not intimacy. As time went by, I began to understand that intimacy not only had nothing to do with sex but was in fact inimical to it. I wrote in *The Ship that Sailed into the Living Room* that sex and intimacy, being antithetical, cannot exist in the same place at the same time; that where one is, the other cannot be. In short, that "sexual intimacy," is an oxymoron.

A couple of Lesbian relationships later, I have had no reason to change my mind.

Now with, Jade, this last and dearest love of my life, I have about as much connectedness with another being as I believe is possible for me in patriarchy, at least partly because we are not sexual—with each other or with anyone else. I don't mean that we have a rule against it. I mean we don't ever feel like it, we're glad to be rid of it, we relish our freedom from it.

But both of us know that what we have together—the passionate tenderness, the fun, the understanding, the desire to be with each other to the end no matter what—though it is wonderful and we are lucky (also definitely still in a relationship, still being sadomasochistic every minute, and still regretting that there is no other way to be together), we know this is not all there is.

We realize now that though true intimacy—the capacity to *be* one another, to know one another as we know ourselves—is not intentionally possible for us in the sadomasochism/hierarchy that is mensworld, it assuredly awaits us in the anarchic female world that is on her way.

Once at a university in the South owned and run by a very conservative church, I conducted a women-only workshop on sex and intimacy the afternoon before my public speech that evening. The Dean of Women attended. After we had all theorized about what the intimacy many of us longed for might be like and what stood in the way of our having it, the Dean shared the following experience with us. (What follows, though not a direct quote, is as true a rendering of her story as I can tell in my own words):

"One summer morning a few years ago, as I stood on a bluff overlooking the Pacific Ocean watching the tide come in, I began to notice a sensation totally unlike anything I'd ever experienced, read, or even heard of before. Beginning in the roots of every hair on my body, it washed across me like an ultra-exquisite orgasm, enveloping my body inside and out.

"As it grew steadily stronger, I felt myself expand to encompass the whole of the scene before me: the ocean surging against the cliffs, its spumes of spray leaping into the air, hanging poised there for a second before crashing down upon the rocks, the trees clinging to the misty hillside, their limbs dancing in the wind. For an unforgettable moment I was all of it—every drop of ocean, every rock, every leaf—quite simply delirious with sensation and life. Stronger and more myself than I had ever been."

"That's it!" I thought. "That's intimacy!"

I am grateful to the Dean of Women for helping me extend my definition of "intimacy" infinitely beyond sex and orgasm (in fact, orgasm as it is achieved and experienced in mensworld hasn't been part of it since.) As she spoke, that word's patriarchal walls collapsed, letting it loose into the universe, sweeping all into its embrace.

Over the years, this vision of intimacy has grown big enough to encompass my dream of a boundless passion, an effortless, spontaneous, joyous connection of one's whole being with all life everywhere, all stars and seas and planets and forests, all plants and animals, all magnificent SisterWitches throughout all universes across all centuries.

Recognizing this experience as possible for me and for all women caused even the best sex to feel puny, contrived, and stultifying. Just downright wrong.

Intimacy isn't something women *have* or *do;* it's not even something that if we're lucky we can experience. Intimacy is what femaleness *is.* It is our SisterWitch heritage, the essence of our entire lost world. If there were only two words we could choose to describe that world (and us, because there was no separation between us and our world), those words would be intimacy and power. But since each of these is essential for the existence of the other, they are not actually separate: intimate-power, intipowermacy, powintermacy.

Over the ensuing years I have come to believe that male sex— the only kind there is in patriarchy, even for Lesbians— has been so totally antithetical to our original way of being that participation in it has left us severely traumatized. So severely, in fact, that many of us can feel almost nothing at all in our bodies. (And all of us are numb in comparison with what is possible for us as females.)

The fathers of the Toxic-Age Movement have added to the damage by indoctrinating women to believe that sex is as natural and necessary to us as it is to men; that, like men, we are sexual beings.

Nothing could be farther from the truth. Maleness is sexuality, femaleness is intimacy—sexuality's polar opposite. But many women have been so successfully sexualized now—for men's benefit, of course—that there is only a small population of females left in the world who have not been seduced by men's lies about sex.

Unfortunately, the thoroughly sexualized woman—the "hot," male-ized woman—figures largely not only in men's wet dreams the world over, but in many Lesbian wet dreams as well. She has even become an ideal of sorts: bravely "in touch" with and expressing her "natural" sexuality. What has not been clear, however, is that the reason more of us are not "in touch" with our sexuality is that, not being innately sexual, we have had to learn from men how to be sexual; then, like all learnings, when we don't intellectually maintain and physically practice it, it dies a natural death. The warning, "use it or lose it," is directed toward women. Men in general need no such exhortation.

For me to suggest that patriarchy's brainwashing machines have deliberately turned women into sex "things"; or to suggest that addiction to sadomasochism's sexual zing absolutely prevents intimacy, is tantamount to confessing that I am a sexually repressed and embittered prude. So be it.

But, I ask women, if sex is so natural for us, why do so many women, Lesbian and otherwise, pay counselors to try to get over their aversion to sex, or just to try to feel like having it?

Well, women answer, it's because of religion, or incest, or rape, or some other sexual desecration, and women seek professional help to try to overcome these traumas enough to be sexually "normal." ("Normal" is in quotation marks because sex is *ab*- normal for females. As Jesse Raven Tree said repeatedly, "Since women and men are opposites, whatever is true for one is totally false for the other.)

Though true, this is not all the truth or perhaps even the largest part of it. That sex is intrinsically boring hardly ever occurs to anyone, even the women who are bored. They simply believe there is something wrong with them.

Because sex is so boring in itself, it needs lots of help, lots of accoutrements, to make it more interesting: alcohol, porn films, bondage equipment, fantasies, whipped cream, and so on and on. For many women who model their behavior on men's, the thrill of the chase, the dance of seduction, not the actual sex act, is what most excites them and, in fact, is often what makes sex possible at all. (That's why so many sexual fantasies include seduction and conquest.) When seduction—that first and headiest part of the ritual—is over (never to return again), the excitation of sex palls. Ultimately this happens with every couple, despite all the propaganda in books, movies, and songs to the contrary.

This propaganda, extolling sex as indescribably transcendent and fulfilling, drowns out the yawns of the millions of women for whom its dreary predictability, its cliched moves, its smallness of vision and narrowness of scope make sex the most boring of all boring activities of patriarchy. And that's very boring indeed!

"Oh, but that's not the way sex is for me!" some protest, adding proudly, "probably because I don't do it like everybody else!"

No matter how original we think we're being, however, even in the exhilarating prelude of seduction and conquest sex is a limited and limiting ritual where every move is prescribed and has been repeated endlessly; this is just as true for overtly sadomasochistic sex as for any other variety. (I say "overtly" because all sex is sadomasochistic, but some people are more interested than others in consciously exploring this mode in bed.) In any kind of sex, there is nothing new under the sun, not even something merely a little tired and shopworn: everything about all varieties of sex is worn out and threadbare.

Therefore, though we may be absolutely convinced that we do sex differently, we are deceiving ourselves. At the very moment we think we are being most original and creative, a billion other people on this planet are doing exactly the same things we are, down to the most minor details.

(That some men have to murder their female sexual partners in order to have an orgasm is not really a divergence from the formula. The ultimate extension of sex—of all sadomasochism—is death. War is a good example of this.)

This is not meant to imply that all sexual behavior comes from the same motives or feelings; it is only to say that worldwide—maybe universally—we all follow pretty much the same sexual means to the same end. Since fucking is essential to men *as a species*, it will always be essential to the patriarchal world.

But it is not essential to women's survival at all; in fact, sex actively threatens it. Still, sex in mensworld has become the only legitimate way to touch another person's body and to have one's own body touched for more than a few seconds at a time. (Except perhaps in medical professions, and body work such as massage. The covert reason many men—and some women—choose these professions, however, has a great deal to do with expanding their access to sex.)

Women need to touch and be touched. As the ones who once lived in a world of unimaginable intimacy with every living being, we need not only physical touching, but touching of all parts of our selves: we need intimacy. Sex, however, by using our bodies as tools, by turning us into "things" for satisfying others, breaks connections and makes intimacy impossible.

Because men perceive all touch as sexual—at the very least, as causing them to think of sex (though according to my former male friends, sex is actually on their minds most of the time)—in patriarchy women have learned to be very careful about touching men. We also know we cannot touch even another woman for any length of time, even to taking her hand as we walk, or hugging her a few seconds past the prescribed hug-time limit, lest we risk being misinterpreted as "coming on" to her. So in a very real sense our need for touching drives us into sexual situations or relationships where touching—of the usual corrupted variety—is both expected and accepted.

Sometimes we hardly notice how starved we are for tenderness, having learned to get by on so little that any at all seems a surfeit. Other than caring for babies and animals and old women, sexual relationships are the only places in mensworld where women can express and receive physical tenderness.

And when sexual relationships fail to satisfy our needs for closeness and connection, as they ultimately will, I wish I could say that we drop our romantic illusions about them and create something else. But these particular illusions are very important to women, a large part of what makes life bearable. They will probably be the last ones to go.

Though many women still want romance and closeness as much as or more than sex in a relationship, others have taken men's cue and are addicted to seduction, needing this impetus for sex as users need drugs. Therefore, when sex palls with one partner, they do what men do: try to find someone new to seduce and conquer or to be seduced and conquered by. (As one male writer wrote in a book years ago, men's egos and libidos need frequent infusions of "strange pussy.") They need a new "thing" to entice into sex, a new will to break, another—and another, and another—conquest. Of course, though all sex is sadomasochism, seduction is a particularly blatant aspect of it, producing as it does a pronounced rush of quasi superiority in the seducer/conqueror.

But afterward, when this first highly-charged phase is over, sex becomes its real self: a very ho-hum sort of business. For women with men, sex becomes not only the definition of predictable and the archetype of boring, but also as deadening as ether.

To sexualize (male-ize) women—i.e., to override our instinctive opposing mode—a good deal of "seasoning" was necessary on the part of our masters-cum-pimps. (By "seasoning" I refer to enslavement tactics—rape, debasement, and torture, for instance—that destroy self-esteem and will.) To make us believe that sex was natural and "empowering" for us, oceans of propaganda flooded—and continue to flood—the media of the Western world.

Before that, it had been obvious to most women that they experienced nothing akin to men's violent sex drive, that the word "sexual" did not mean the same for them as it did for men, that it did not figure centrally in their lives as it did in men's, and that, in fact, it played such a different role that the word "sex" could not be said to adequately represent both women and men.

Men knew the difference, of course, none better, so—at least in the English language—they were careful to supply no word that would give credence to this difference, no language with which to *think* it and to think *about* it. Having to share the word "sexual" with men encouraged us to believe that we also shared their sexual reality.

But some of us—those whose strong female energy men most craved—were slow to come around. We still remembered intimacy.

Though men care nothing about intimacy themselves, never having been able to experience it—as we can see from their behavior—they have always known that women have the capacity for it (whatever it is), that we need it, and that we long for it. So they cleverly "solved" this problem.

Owning the language and defining words whenever necessary to maintain privilege and control— in this case specifically to ensure our participation in sex—they simply declared sex and intimacy synonymous. In doing this, they immeasurably strengthened their ongoing campaign to open the floodgates of women's life-energy wider yet, giving themselves even greater access.

Language is one of men's best friends.

Having persuaded us to accept that sex was intimacy and as "natural" for women as it was for men, the Toxic-Age fathers turned the screw one last thread: they inaugurated a brilliantly diabolical and hugely successful brainwashing program to persuade us that sex is also "sacred," an exalted form of spirituality. Hardly a surprise. Everything men are, do, need, and believe is decreed "sacred." There is no other meaning for sacred in this world of theirs.

Because we have been programmed to believe that men and women are the same in essence, and because women's female essence is so loving, trusting, and honest, we unconsciously project these female qualities onto men and believe even men's most outrageous lies—such as everything they tell us about sex.

(That we project our own natures upon men makes us pushovers for them, and believe me, they are fully aware of this, having used it against us from their beginnings. Their knowledge that this predilection of ours for "oneness" will prevent us from recognizing and believing their true motives gives them enormous advantage over us. An advantage they never hesitate to take.

Then, by our never failing to fall for their lies, by always meeting their expectations that we will be complete patsies, we continually reinforce and encourage their deception—and their contempt for us. Men smirk, "What fools women are! How easy to control! Just say love, just say peace, just say unity, and their legs fairly fly apart for us!")

At their beginnings, some men did observe that women lived every moment in the kind of intimacy the Dean of Women described. But because they could never experience it themselves, could never be female in any way (as opposed to feminine), and could therefore never understand it, men interpreted it in the context of their own sexual natures and concluded that women were sexually insatiable.

A world of difference exists between being sexually insatiable and experiencing total intimacy with all living things every moment.

But intimacy, as unlike sex as anything is possible to be, requires, first of all, absolute equality. This rules out intimacy with men, since no woman experiences equality in the sex act no matter what she believes. Inequality is, quite simply, the basis of sexual intercourse (and of all male sex even when it is taking place between two women, though it can be considerably less pronounced).

Second, intimacy is dependent upon integrity. Therefore, anything that requires physical or emotional manipulation or pretence of any sort (as sex always does for women) instantly sabotages intimacy. We disconnect spiritually from ourselves and from our sexual partner, for instance, when to please her we moan, or murmur, "Oh, that's so good, yes, yes!" when the feeling is not truly moan-worthy.

Or when we writhe and squirm and pump our pelvis and grab her rump and bite her neck to prove that we're really excited when we often are only mildly so, if at all. But as we all know, much of this is really just part of the sex "act." No matter how genuinely we care about someone else, sex is always a performance, our "part" so well memorized and so often practiced that we perceive it every time as just coming naturally.

But in every sexual interlude of our lives, we pretend more pleasure than we actually feel. (Studies have proved this to be the case with women, but I didn't need them to tell me that and I'll bet you didn't, either.) Sex cannot occur without dozens of instances of deceit, large and small. Dishonesty is simply a tacit, universally accepted, requirement of sex.

But anytime we fake pleasure in any way—as we cannot avoid doing in sex, and not just faking orgasm—we evict integrity from our presence. Since power is dependent upon integrity, when integrity goes, so does power, and we become as weak as men.

So we are weak whenever we use others' bodies to reach any goal, such as to feel victorious in seduction, or to feel secure and loved or to make our partner feel secure or loved, or to have an orgasm, or to establish ownership/partnership rights, or to keep our lover from leaving us, or to prove our sexual prowess by manipulating someone to have—or at least to pretend to have—a puny little orgasm. ("Puny" describes even the strongest and longest orgasm compared with our infinite female capacity for pleasure.)

Since it is not an activity, intimacy, unlike sex, cannot be aligned with any goal. Since it is not an activity, it cannot exist in means-to-ends, stimulus-response behavior such as sex.

Back when I first began differentiating between sex and intimacy, I so longed for intimacy that I was determined to find a route to it somehow through patriarchy's maze of blockades. I knew that, unlike sex, intimacy is one hundred percent female, based on integrity and therefore full of power.

I hypothesized, therefore, that if we honored and enjoyed each touch for itself alone, if we never debased it by using it as a bridge to the next touch along the same old road to the same old orgasm; that is, if our every touch were honestly only what it seemed to be, not a means to some end other than being enjoyable in itself right at this moment; if we were not pretending pleasure with the touch of the moment while actually planning the next move and how to use it to move closer to the goal; if we could completely trust one another not to touch in this sex mode, perhaps, I thought, we could be intimate right now, even in patriarchy.

But no.

As we began our sex/intimacy experiment, Jade and I were dismayed to find that when we touched without sexual purpose—i.e, without flipping on our sex switch and focusing on having an orgasm—our skin felt hardly anything at all, as if it were covered with a thick protective covering. We concluded that our bodies had been used for so long as means to the end of libidinous gratification that it might take them a long time to drop their guard, to let themselves be sensuously vulnerable. So touching without a goal, without sadomasochism, was probably going to feel very boring for awhile.

And we were right—it did.

Gradually, though, as we persisted in our no-ulterior-motive touching, our bodies began to trust and finally shed their second thick skin, and *felt*. Now, after nineteen years of this, we are so sensitive and responsive that goose bumps and chills often flood over us at the slightest touch. Though we cannot deliberately experience intimacy—i.e., *being* one another—we at least lessen the sadomasochistic gulf between us, coming much closer to equality and the truth of femaleness than is possible in sex.

Because intimacy is not linear, not like sex: now your mouth (pant), now your breast (pant, pant), now your vulva (pant, pant, pant)—in short, because intimacy is not sadomasochistic, not male—women cannot experience it in the patriarchs' paradigm except in serendipitous, brief, and heretical flashes. And though it seems ironic that we are least likely to experience it while engaged in sex, intimacy cannot be *made* to happen. It is one hundred percent spontaneous.

And exceedingly rare.

Unlike sex, intimacy is not something women *do*; it is what we *are*. It is the female way of being in the world. Females of every species are intimate, not sexual, beings. We have been programmed to have sex and to find it natural and inexorable only because it is necessary for men's survival.

Females, however, being the opposite of males, are capable of incalculable pleasure and connection with our entire selves—bodies, emotions, spirits—not just our genitalia, and for countless reasons in countless ways. This is what we have remembered (albeit more and more dimly) and have always tried to find in sex.

This is why we have always been disappointed.

But to enjoy sex in any way as men do, as they tell us we should if we want to be fully-functioning human beings (though of course we are not human beings at all), we have to narrow down our perceptions, close down our senses instead of expanding them to include the ocean, cliffs, and trees—these would be distractions. We have to reduce our expectations, numb down those parts of our bodies that our sexual partners, male or female, typically take no interest in—which is most of them (but what about *me!* cries the elbow)—and concentrate intently on the few *important* ones. We may even have to include a sadomasochistic fantasy in our warm-up routine to generate enough excitation to proceed.

Sometimes, in the middle of all this, I used to see, not only how thoroughly lacking in integrity sex is, but also how ludicrous. Back in my early Lesbian days, for instance, here my love and I are, lying in bed talking, my head on her shoulder, my arm across her stomach, her hand stroking my hair, when suddenly I realize that her hand has dropped to my upper arm and that the touch has now changed, is slower, more deliberate, and occasionally allows her arm to brush my breast.

Ah. She is asking whether I'm available for sex. I check in with my body while her fingers leave my arm and settle on my nipple. Okay, I think, it's been awhile. I guess I can do it.

So I flip on my sex switch and begin concentrating on the task at hand. Finally, we are in position: our t-shirts off, upper-body foreplay all taken care of, her with her lower legs and feet now hanging off the end of the bed while the rest of her smothers beneath the winter blanket, and me with my head and neck scrunched up against the headboard clutching the blanket to my freezing chest.

Ready now for the Big Moment: the mouth-to-clitoris connection.

For the next while, both of us do our best to create between us some sexual excitation. I focus fervently on trying to feel something interesting in my vulva, and am just about succeeding when the phone rings. And rings. And rings. We pretend we are too enraptured to hear it. But of course the mood—what there was of it—is totally disrupted, so in exasperation I spring up to unplug the phone.

When I return to bed, her face emerges, red and perspiring, from under the blanket and we give each other raised-eyebrow looks that ask silently whether or not we think we can recapture enough of our hard-won feeling to make it worthwhile to go on, or whether we should give it up for the night.

I'm tired and not interested anymore but for the sake of the relationship (whoops! If we hadn't evicted integrity before this, we do it now), we both agree to continue. She disappears under the blanket again and I resume my position.

But now the situation is even tenser than before. She's been cramped and breathless under there so long that I feel great guilty urgency to get this orgasm underway.

So now I concentrate in earnest, I *seriously* focus.

"Don't think of anything else," I command myself. "Just focus. Gather up every feeling you can from everywhere and direct it to your vulva. Quick! Come on now, focus!"

Something a little tingly starts "down there," and I cross my fingers that no friend rings the doorbell, or that I won't sneeze or fart—that nothing will happen to interrupt this mounting sensation.

Focus, focus!

Thank goodness, nothing untoward does happen and I do finally manage the requisite orgasm. But I can never be sure which I enjoy more: the orgasm itself or the relief that I managed to do it before my lover suffocated

At this point, I just wish it were over and we could cuddle down to sleep, but there is still work to be done. It's my turn to swelter under the blanket and hers to work her way to orgasm. I heave a sigh, and get on with it.

At other times, we try different positions, different venues, different approaches. But no matter what we try, sex takes work, it takes *doing,* and sometimes considerable doing. It doesn't just happen spontaneously all over our bodies and throughout our spirits because of the glorious power of life that abounds in and around us.

Not only does it *not* make us "one," as the Dean became with the California coast, it doesn't even live up to its far smaller billing of being pleasurable from start to finish (except, perhaps at the very beginning of a relationship or encounter when typically a sizeable s/m rush is easier to achieve and maintain).

Despite the massive propaganda upholding and surrounding it, however, and the astounding frequency with which it is taking place, sex seems to be living up to its promise even less than usual. So, as I say earlier, almost the only way remaining for men to raise their global sexual/sadomasochistic ante, now that they have wars raging across the planet and have loosed sickness, misery, and death upon all nations, is to blow the world to smithereens.

Well, women ask, if sex is not good for women, what's the alternative? Celibacy?

This is when I tell them about non-sexual, *almost*-intimate touch. I tell them even though I know that those who haven't reached these conclusions on their own will very likely find this sort of touching anticlimactic (!) and boring, not an alternative at all. Still, writing about it here gives me a chance to catch, and perhaps to share, the barest glimpse of the female world again.

An exquisite closeness is possible in loving a woman without exploiting her for sex. Touching her without a goal, without trying to manipulate her into feeling anything—in fact, without *thinking* about how she feels; without *having* to think about it. Because both of you understand and agree upon what you are trying to do, she will tell you honestly if she doesn't want you to continue. Like you, she expects to be responsible only for her own feelings and behavior.

So you touch her simply because to touch her is so sweet to your hand, to your stomach, to your arms, so like touching yourself, so stirring to your memory of women's world where intimacy with every living thing was the order of our days.

Such an experience requires that you touch your lover's body when you genuinely want only that touch and nothing else. You touch an elbow, for instance, because that elbow stirs your heart: her small, strong, finely articulated bones, the supple layer of delicate skin covering her fascia, tendons, and muscles, the whole of her so full of intelligence, spirit, and humor. Because you never touch her in preparation for touching some other body part next, you never dishonor the elbow in your hand. Or your lover.

All the time you are focused on this elbow (or this back, or this leg), your lover knows you are enjoying yourself. Because you both understand that to pretend interest when you have none destroys integrity, she knows that the moment you have touched all you want to, you will stop. So she doesn't need to worry that you may be getting tired or bored and that she needs to offer to "take her turn" now and touch you.

Trusting you to do only what you want to do, she also knows she doesn't have to respond—make noises or movements—to manipulate you to continue. She can relax, even go to sleep if she wants, and you will not only not be offended but may not even notice. Her elbows (her knees, her hair, her legs)—not her reaction to your touch—will remain your focus.

I'm sure many women have discovered that arms are veritable pleasure-troves. Gently squeezing their muscles up and down their length, licking and nibbling them, caressing them lightly, slowly on their seemingly millions of nerve endings—these touches simply take one's breath away. Arms have as much pleasure potential as any of the supposedly "sexual" parts.

Speaking of sexual parts, when on occasion we are able to outwit our sex minds, the vulva and breasts can be touched, explored, and loved in the same non-sexual way as the feet and shoulders.

So the practice is simple: touching without the intent to use—that is, without psychological coercion, with neither physical nor emotional manipulation. Touching the breasts, the hands, the face, the stomach, the anything without flipping the sex switch—i.e., without attempting to feel sexually excited or to stimulate excitation in another.

Because this is genuinely respectful and full of integrity, it contributes hugely to emotional and physical health. There is also pleasure, closeness, and trust in it, and wonderful talk, laughter, word games, and other stuff. Being so inclusive, so honest, it offers a whiff of intimacy and women's world.

Now I can hear someone saying, "But I have talk and laughter and other stuff with sex!" "During it?" "Well, not usually; at the beginning or after we're through." Just as I thought: sex is serious business and demands lots of concentration. And notice the word "through." We get "through" with sex; it ends.

The intimacy that is femaleness—and that is on her way—never falters but lasts forever.

Unfortunately we also get "through" with the touching I've been describing, because it is trapped in patriarchy and cannot fly free of its particularity, its minuscule scope, its "doingness," its *time*. But now that it's over for the night, you fall asleep in a kiss. You can do this because what you have been about here is not a sacred ritual, there is no specified decorum, no rigid protocol for it as there is for sex that says you must act interested and perky to the bitter end. Touching in this non-sadomasochistic way is not the serious business sex is because, unlike sex, it is not necessary for the preservation of male control.

Instead, insofar as it is somewhat non-paradigmatic, it is a threat to male control. Through it we can remember and access a little of our power; perhaps this is why so many Lesbians have discovered and are practicing it. Whatever the case, fortunately, this mode of touching is intellectually invisible to men, so entirely unimaginable that they don't even know it exists. The potential for equality, for integrity and power in female intimacy . . . this is what men so feared when they emerged on our planet and encountered us; this is what they so feared that finally, through rape, torture, murder—the usual—they overrode our natural impulse for intimacy and replaced it with male sexuality.

The intimacy that women were before maleness was never an activity, but instead an enormously powerful way of being. Though in comparison to real intimacy, non-sexual touching seems almost as vague and elusive as the memory of a scent, it is still the physically closest we can come to it now.

But I do not mean to disparage it. That such touching is possible to any degree in patriarchy is amazing, miraculous. It is heresy, a highly seditious declaration of independence from sexual slavery, women's lot in patriarchy. However, the power—the intimacy and gloriousness of it, its constancy—will have to wait for the return of the female universe.

Of course, there's no sense trying to touch in this way with men. They cannot do it, nor can imagine wanting to. First and foremost, men are sadomasochistic beings, sexual beings. Even while feeling the elbow or the knee, sooner rather than later they will have an erection. They can't help it, and there is no sense tormenting them.

Women have told me that men pretend to like simple touching, they say men can do it for awhile, but they admit that men have to have sex and if forced to have elbows even once in awhile will turn to other women for sex and never touch an elbow again. So most parts of heterosexual women's bodies will have to go to the grave unnoticed, untouched, and unloved.

Though such touching is possible for any two women, whether they call themselves Lesbians or not, probably even most feminists will not be interested in elbows either. Participation in such an experiment as this requires not only an interest in the workings of patriarchy, but also a fierce and unquenchable desire to escape hierarchy/sadomasochism as much as is womanly possible. It takes time and patience; it takes not accepting men's ubiquitous and iniquitous lies about sex; it takes believing in one's own anti-conventional experience, and in the thousands of other women's who have stumbled upon it.

But since these are not common concerns among women of any sexual orientation, the odds are poor that as long as maleness exists non-sexual touching will ever attain the status of an alternative to male sex. Until maleness is gone from the universe, most women who have a choice will continue to opt for sex: its familiarity comforts them. They and any possible partners know how to do it. The fact that almost everyone else on the planet is doing it reassures them that it is as things were "meant to be." Not least important is that it beats being marooned—untouched and aching for closeness—in the affectional desert men have made of the world.

I've been there and I sympathize.

Like them, I have felt that there was always a chance that next time sex would touch my heart and ease my loneliness, that next time it would be worth it. That in the sea of bitterness called patriarchy, next time a wave of sweetness might break over me like the sweetness of my dimly remembered dream world.

But it never happened.

Still, there were many lovely moments in my Lesbian sexual life, enough that when integrity would no longer allow me to do sex, I was lost and very frightened, afraid my male-inculcated belief that all touch was sexual would turn out to be true and that I would never again in all my life be able to touch or be touched. I didn't see how I could continue to live if that happened. I couldn't even imagine wanting to live.

Then I heard that Jesse Raven Tree had once said something about touching a woman, not for its effect on *her*, but for its effect on *oneself*. And, astonished and overjoyed, I recognized at once that this was the piece I had been looking for, the non-manipulative, non-controlling, non-sadomasochistic piece that would allow me to go on living. I was in love with this premise and expected to be able to step completely out of patriarchy on the strength of it.

This was totally unrealistic of me, of course. But my enthusiasm didn't wane even during the first few years of experimentation while I groped about not really understanding what I was doing. All I knew to do was to give my faith to some more honest way of being and to the search for intimacy whether or not it could ever be found in mensworld.

Well, I understand a great deal more now, and am glad that when I wanted to die because I could see no way to be touched without sadomasochism, my eternally springing hope (and my curiosity) forced me to keep trying. Though I know that the touching I have described will have to suffice until maleness and sex are gone from the universe and femaleness and intimacy return, I cannot convey in men's feeble language how hugely and eagerly my every cell and nerve ending await that day!

PART V

The SisterWitch Conspiracy

Chapter 15

The SisterWitch Promise

In the deepening dusk of a summer evening in the year 1599, women gather on a hillside outside the market town of Wheathampstead, England. They talk quietly among themselves about the women who are absent, the ones who have already been tortured and killed in these burning times. Though they all agree that the spirits of these women are with them here tonight, they confess how terribly they miss seeing them, speaking with them, kissing their soft cheeks, holding them in their arms. Looking sadly out over the hillside, they mourn for all that is lost, remembering the many times that more than two hundred women gathered here, the hillside alive with their passion and courage.

Tonight they count thirty women sitting in their circle. "Only thirty of us left," they shiver, and move closer together.

One at a time now, these remaining women rise and speak what is in their hearts: they entreat one another never to forget what they know about their world before men, who they were, who they still most quintessentially are. Remember, they say, this is our work: in the face of unspeakable violence, to *remember*; despite everything men do life after life to destroy our memories of ourselves, to be fierce in our determination to remember.

And to be faithful in reminding one another.

Standing straight and proud and beautiful in the starlight, their faces shining with power, they speak of their great love for one another; they bless one another with the strength and courage to meet the terrible fate that is even now bearing down upon them. They know there will not be time to meet here again, and that they are unlikely to meet one another anywhere again in this life.

When they have all spoken, they form smaller circles and sit close together on the ground. Across these circles, they clasp hands and under the starry sky, with owls calling softly around them, each makes a promise to the others:

"I, Molly, covenant with you, my beloved sisters, that when men's time is over, I will meet you again. I promise that I will be here on this planet to help re-create our female world and walk into it with you, hand in hand."

In the starlight, tears glisten down her cheeks as she looks from face to face, then adds quietly, "I am your sister forever. I will never forget you, never forsake you, never stop loving you."

Then another woman speaks, and another, and another:

"Dearest sisters, I, Eleanor, also covenant that I will be here when our time comes again, to do whatever I can do, be whatever I need to be, to restore our world. I covenant with you that between that time and this I will remember you, I will love you steadfastly, I will be true to our purpose. You can trust these words."

As they go around the circle, all the terrible fear and grief and horror they have been feeling—knowing they will soon suffer the fate of their sisters—falls from their hearts and they are filled with hope and love and a sure knowledge that this will not be their last meeting, that at patriarchy's end they will meet again to re-emerge together as the female world.

They also find comfort in knowing that they are not alone; that in addition to being surrounded by their countless female allies in the spirit realms, they are in the presence of the spirits of living women like themselves, not only from England and Europe, but from all over the world, who remember what they remember, who face the same fate they now face—their true sisters though they have never met. They are heartened by the knowledge that these women have made the same covenants with one another as they themselves have made this night.

The women on the hillside also know that these distant women, aware of their existence here in England, have entered into this covenant with *them* as well as with women everywhere. All these amazing women, still preserving some memory of their power, promising one another across continents, across oceans, as women had promised for thousands of years before them, "I will come to you at the end of men's world. Believe in me. Wait for me."

The slaughter of the witches of which they were part, this concentrated centuries-long global massacre of nine million European women and at least twelve million more on other continents, terrorized us as nothing previously had managed to do. This time, men's attempt to break women's connection, the connection that was—and is—our power, was largely successful. Profoundly traumatized and afraid for our lives, we denied and renounced our female power, hiding it from ourselves and others in the deep background for the next four hundred years—right up to our time—where it remains today.

But in the final years of the 16th century, in the English hills, in the deserts, on the mountaintops, by the streams, on the shores of the seas, in the jungles and forests, in the caves behind the waterfalls, women everywhere, *safe from men's eyes,* whispered in one another's ears, sang aloud, called to one another's hearts across the vastnesses of the world: "Remember me!"

Perhaps some of us were on that hillside in Wheathampstead. But if we were not part of that particular community, any woman who has read this far can be certain she was in some circle like it somewhere in the world, promising that she would remember us, that no matter what men did to her, she would never stop loving us, and that she would be there with all of us at patriarchy's end.

And here we are at last—at just the right time, the time we've awaited for ages—certain that our presence is not accidental. We know we have promises to keep, promises we *must* keep.

What are women's covenants that they have kept such urgency alive in us for hundreds of years?

The root of both "covenant" and "coven," men's word books say, is the Latin word "convenire" meaning to convene or come together. However, some of these books go on to expand the definition of "coven" to include its being also a meeting of confederates with a secret plan and agenda—as in a gathering of witches.

I choose to think of the word "covenant," when used by women, as derived from "coven." In our covens since the beginning of patriarchy we not only engaged in rituals where we remembered together what femaleness is and who we really are, we also made solemn promises to one another and to the planet. Coven-ant, therefore, is a word so full of femaleness that as a word it is not only highly appropriate, but also powerful and accurate enough to fit the women we were in those circles four hundred years ago. We were confederates, and we did have a secret plan and agenda. (We still do, of course. Gathering some fragments of it here is part of a global effort to mend our terrific disconnection from one another.)

A coven-ant among women would therefore be a *female* promise, as different in its meaning from the mere word "promise" as femaleness is from maleness. A promise in patriarchy, particularly a spoken promise, is so morally insubstantial and of such little value that more often than not it can be casually broken. Promises of the sort commonly made in mensworld, even though they may be called "covenants"—as they are in the mormon church and other religious sects—are assumed to be breakable the moment they become difficult or inconvenient. (Mormons make very male "covenants" in their temples, promising to disembowel themselves, or slice their throats rather than reveal what they just experienced there—activities and teachings so jejune that they in no way merit these or any other such extreme and histrionic sacrifices.)

On the other hand, covenants such as those we made with one another at Wheathampstead at the end of the 16th century were based in metaethical power, binding on us, therefore, to the end of time and beyond. Central to women's secret resistance movement that dates from the first years of maleness and still survives in us, these covenants have been necessary only during our patriarchal captivity and have been made exclusively between and among women.

Our promises are unbreakable, not because we would have faced external repercussions if we had broken them, but because we understood the relationship of integrity to power—in fact, of the absolute necessity of integrity to power and hence the absolute necessity of keeping faith with one another if we were ever to restore femaleness.

We kept these covenants also because we valued and respected one another as women. No, more than that: because we adored one another, because we cherished all that was female.

Many women have told me in the last few years that they know there is a reason for them to be alive now, a few even perceiving women's destiny as I do. But though most do not share my interpretation of things, any woman who feels and believes that she must now survive *no matter what* is a member of the Sisterhood I am describing.

That *is* what I am describing, of course: a rebirth of our deep feelings of sisterhood, our eternal connection. After many long lonely years, we have fulfilled the first part of our promise to the women we once loved: we are here, meeting again across this globe and on every planet throughout the universe. We may not be aware that we are finding those whose hands we clasped across some circle somewhere hundreds of years ago, but every so often we *are* finding them. And not by accident.

Of course, not every woman we meet is someone we once knew and cared about, and many women we have never met before will ultimately join us with whole hearts even when our former friends will not. But even if we recognized which ones were which, we would find that we do not like some of our old friends very much now, after what they and we have become in the years since we last met, that some of us have suffered in ways and to degrees that seem to have made deep, positive feelings about femaleness impossible.

Nevertheless, nothing can change the fact that any of us who were rebels in other lives and who have chosen to be alive now have thus far been true to one another and to femaleness.

We did more in Wheathampstead than covenant that we would be here on time, however; we also agreed to help with whatever needed to be done. So those of us who are still im-passioned about a female world are trying to fulfill that part of our promise, re-affirming our vow to stand fast with one another now through the perilous winding down of men's paradigm, renewing our coven-ant to do whatever we can see to do.

Since we have been moving resolutely toward this time and this crucial re-union for centuries, it seems reasonable to believe that we not only knew *when* we needed to meet again, but that somewhere within us we know *why* we are here, we know *what* to do, and we know *how* to do it.

All that is necessary is to encourage this information—gently tug it—out of our unconscious minds, trusting the power of our love for one another and for the female universe to continue to illuminate our homeward path.

Chapter 16

Our Planet, Our Selves

Many of us say that we are gravely affected by watching Earth's agonizing decline at men's hands. We say we would do anything to stop it. But how far does "anything" mean we are prepared to go?

Our beautiful planet is fighting for her life. Though the choice of the word "fighting" may offend some women, it has the merit of being accurate: men are waging an all-out war against her, as they are against all femaleness. In this life-or-death struggle, Earth is besieged now on every flank, desperately trying to survive.

Evil of the magnitude that she—and we—are facing is so daunting that we are hard pressed to think of more than small ways to mitigate it—i.e., recycling, conserving water, planting gardens and trees. Hundreds of years ago when we promised to be here at this time, we neither could have foreseen nor imagined what a horrifying, colossal mess we would be walking into. Nevertheless, here we are with our willing hearts, ready to do our part.

Our planet, our sisters, we ourselves—all of us now need even more vital female energy than usual to offset men's skyrocketing use of it as they and their systems struggle not to shut down. But how can we generate more when we often feel as if we have barely enough to fuel our own lives?

One sure way is to remember that, because all females, including Planet Earth, are literally one, we directly influence one another with our every breath. This means, for instance, that since she feels what we feel, our planet receives a wave of hope and comfort whenever we feel hopeful and at peace with ourselves. It means that whatever passion and joy we feel about ourselves and our sisters *as females* not only includes her but strengthens her own passionate female life force. It means that the good we do one another as women rejuvenates and heartens her, too. Through us, Earth experiences the powerful female energy we generate when we deal kindly, generously, and respectfully with ourselves and other women. Like us, she thrives in this atmosphere.

Therefore, we can magnify our power and energy a thousand-fold by putting at the top of our list of priorities the absolute necessity of treating women as respectfully and honorably as we can, and demanding the same treatment in return. We must commit to doing this whether or not we like a particular woman or would choose her for a friend. When we overcome our massive woman-hatred enough to do this—and we are going to have to give it our best try, beginning immediately—we will know that we can meet with equanimity any challenge the future holds for us.

Being able to perceive most women as admirable and to treat all women with respect is without doubt the most difficult, the most seditious, and therefore the most female-power-generating behavior in the patriarchal world. To create the quiet hurricane of female energy that will enable us to do this now, we actually have no choice but to face and if not conquer, at least subdue, the fierce misogyny we have learned from being oppressed because of our gender; the misogyny feminists call "internalized oppression."

When I was actively rearing four children, on the refrigerator in my kitchen hung a reminder that was very popular among mothers in the '60's and '70's, entitled, "Children Learn What They Live." The list of examples that followed included:

If children live with love, they learn to love themselves and others.
If children live with respect, they learn to respect
themselves and others.
If children live with kindness, they learn to be
kind to themselves and others.

But unlike little boys, little girls, from the time we emerge
from the womb, are denied the best of these self-esteem-
building responses from others. Instead, we are beset at once
and on every level of our lives by profoundest disrespect. This
manifests, in part, as objectification (what use is she? what can
she do to justify her existence? how can she meet our needs?),
lack of positive attention, ridicule, intolerance, outright physical and verbal assault, second-class love.

If little girls don't experience this abuse in their immedi-
ate families—though very few escape it—they most certainly
and always experience it everywhere else. Every baby girl born
into patriarchy, regardless of her particular situation, learns
quickly and is never allowed to forget that she is inferior to
the boys of her race and class (and any other category she may
have been assigned by birth) because she is female.

This is the bane, and the tragedy, of all females everywhere:
that we have ineluctably internalized the inferiority that males
of all races, classes, and nationalities assign us at birth; that
this has left its indelible mark upon our self-esteem no matter
what we have achieved in life; and that we project our feelings
about ourselves—and our fury at the unbearable unfairness of
it all—upon other females.

So living from our first moment to our last in a closed
system of female inferiority, an inescapable cage of woman-
hatred called sexism, it is no wonder we learn to hate ourselves and other inferior ones like us, treating ourselves and

other women with disrespect, impatience, anger, intolerance, unkindness, objectification, and all the rest of it.

As my refrigerator door reminded me every day: we learn what we live. Ergo, oppressed people learn to oppress.

Woman-hating, being endemic to patriarchy—actually being a huge part of its definition—is deeply embedded in all of us. Therefore, as long as men exist, our being able to love and respect *totally* the femaleness of ourselves and other women is highy unlikely.

But what is not impossible—and will substitute very well—is, as much as we can, to act as if we do. By "acting as if," we can momentarily bypass our internal oppression and help generate the life-sustaining energy so necessary to us now. We can do this—at least much of the time—and it will be enough.

We really can, for instance, resist the terrific temptation to be negative about or speak against other women behind their backs or to confront them with rage. This may sound simple, but every one of us knows it is not. Since men have always rewarded us for attacking other women, this behavior has become one of our strongest temptations. Men have perfected this and other tactics to turn us against one another—to break our connection and diffuse our power—while pretending to be our best friends, our caring "brothers."

But we can refuse to fall for their divide-and-conquer ploys, and each time we do—each time we resist the almost overwhelming sadomasochistic urge to trash some other woman or group of women to get a hit of illusory superiority—we give an enormous boost to the creation of female energy and connection everywhere.

Because this acting-as-if energy redounds to bless all females, including our planet, treating women kindly, non-hierarchically (i.e., non-condescingly), tolerantly, and—

when we honestly feel it—affectionately, sends a tsunami of women's energy around the world; it is powerful activism.

This does not mean that we allow ourselves to be abused or mistreated by other women in order to "keep the peace"; respecting ourselves and other women means we tell one another the truth—as kindly as we can, but also as clearly as we can. Pollyanna was neither an honest nor an honorable model for women. Bravely and kindly confronting behavior that hurts us, honestly and bravely listening when others confront us kindly about our behavior, and then doing whatever we can to stop giving or receiving pain—this has always been necessary for true friendship.

When we sincerely try to act as if femaleness is worthy of our respect, whether we are totally successful every time or not, we thumb our noses at our internalized oppression enough to create an energy that fortifies, invigorates, and helps heal Earth and all females everywhere. Acting as if we find femaleness pretty wonderful—as it is exemplified in our own loving behavior—is not only central to the planet's survival and the survival of all women, but is also the only truly revolutionary act that has ever been possible for women in patriarchy, and the only one now open to us.

Our planet needs us to go even beyond this, however; she needs some very specifically physical "acting as if" to generate a very physical kind and quality of energy: She needs our commitment to stay here beside her in our bodies to the end, if we can, or for as long as we can.

We might wonder why this is necessary. Certainly the non-embodied women in the spirit realms can also create—are creating—enormous energy for Earth's survival. Since females are equally efficient energy generators in any form, why the very compelling inner voice insisting that it is necessary for as many of us as possible to remain here in the flesh until men are gone?

Perhaps it is because Earth is being attacked in her body and it is her body she is struggling to save that the particular energy of our bodies is the energy she most needs now.

She is also spirit, of course, and despite her long physical travail, is still strong in spirit. While it is true that her body and spirit are not separate, it is also true that her body, like ours, contributes a very specific and essential body/matter-based energy to the total entity that she is; a unique power that, despite her strong spirit, is being consumed rapidly in her extraordinarily strenuous physical efforts to fend off men's attacks.

I have heard many women say, "They cannot kill the planet; she is too strong for them." I wish this were true. While men can never kill her spirit—like all female spirits, hers is immortal—they can destroy her body just as they can ours. Even as I write these words they are demonstrating in countless ways not only that they can destroy her but also that they want and intend to.

So our lover, Earth, trying to save her marvelous body, now needs our bodies to be here alongside hers, generating this essential body-energy, this unique body-power. Even under siege, she is generating much of the energy she needs. But not enough, and maybe not for long enough. She is in critical need of emergency infusions of life energy. And so are we. Males, now needing to consume more female energy than ever before to do less than ever before, are draining it out of the universe faster than all female entities are able to replenish it.

Not more or faster than we *can*, however. Since we *can* generate more, it seems to me that we *must*, or at least must try to do everything we can to raise the specifically female energy the planet needs and in amounts sufficient to thwart men's attempts to destroy her.

We can consciously energize our beautiful planet in simple, direct ways. With every step of our feet upon her skin, we can send loving female energy into her body. We can lie next to her, let our love for her flow directly and powerfully from our heart into hers. We can ply her with affection and appreciation, consciously, many times a day.

We can regard and treat her as an equal, neither a goddess to be worshipped (she is female, and therefore an-archic) nor a mother-servant, here solely for our benefit, solely to meet our needs. She is more than and different from either: she is our peer, our lover, one of our dearest, most steadfast friends.

As her friends and lovers, we can promise her that we will not abandon her, but will remain by her side—if at all possible—until the end of mensworld and the end of her travail. Through all this, we can open to her the energy of our hearts and lives, demonstrate that it is hers to use, hers to take whenever she needs it. In the ways I have suggested and that follow—and any others we can think of—we can offer her our female strength rather than sit back passively as it is sucked out of us by male institutions and systems. We are strong enough for this, strong enough to lift from her a little of the burden of generating the physical energy so essential to her now.

In our frequent conversations with her, we can tell her how passionately we want her to survive now in her current body, the body we have known and loved so well for so long. Though we know her spirit will never die and can always be re-embodied, this is the body we want to be with when patriarchy is gone. For who can be sure that such a marvelous body as hers can ever be duplicated? At this moment, she is the most magnificent planet in the universe.

But how can we truthfully say all this, how can we share our own physical energy with her if we are depleting it through our faulty physical habits? Where is the integrity of telling her we genuinely love her body when we hate ours? We may not be totally aware that this is how we feel about ourselves, but we have not lived under men's woman-hating regime for thousands of years without being deeply imprinted by it in multitudes of ways.

As we know all too well, theirs is a regime in which the brain is perceived and revered as male, while the body is perceived and loathed as female. Patriarchy is a regime in which men treat brain-intelligence as the noblest of all assets—because it is all they have—and body-intelligence as nonexistent—because it is nonexistent in them. A regime in which they therefore systematically destroy the bodies of every species (2,000 Amazon Forest trees a second), including their own, in horrific ways every day. A regime under which female bodies are so savagely envied, feared, and hated that they are reserved for men's utmost cruelty.

Universally, they degrade our bodies to things whose primary function is to satisfy their insatiable appetites for sex and control; they turn us into the breeders and servants of their species, making us pay for their humiliation at being so absolutely dependent upon us when they are so totally nonessential to us.

Being thus unremittingly oppressed—i.e., sexually abused—because of our female bodies, almost all of us, whether we are conscious of it or not, feel that our bodies are inferior specimens. From men's abuse springs serious self-abuse (we learn what we live): addictions, such as starving, bingeing, purging, cutting, drugging, etc., as well as cosmetic attacks like face lifts, stomach tucks, the lopping off of unwanted lumps here and the adding of silicone or saline lumps there—self-hating and -defeating strategies in our battle to feel better about being female in patriarchy.

I understand this powerful impulse from my own life. Fifty years ago I married someone whose friends teased him about being a "breast-and-ankle" man. Since I had very small breasts and so-so ankles, why he married me is anyone's guess. Then about halfway through our marriage, he took me to a science fair at Stanford University to show me the latest marvel: silicone breast implants! Wouldn't I love a couple?

This pressure so built upon the shame I had always felt as a lesser woman in my padded bras that shortly thereafter I had Dow-Corning breast implants installed on my chest. That's how they felt: like things to be installed, as alien and lifeless as brake shoes. But I liked having a more desirable shape; I liked being able to find a bra that fit. So I tolerated them.

Then, ironically, years after I became buxom, I discovered feminism and suffered the reverse shame of being a silicone-enhanced feminist. Finally, guilt, added to my fear for my health, compelled me to have the brake shoes removed.

I could say that then I was myself again, but I was certainly not the "myself" I would have been without two serious—and totally unnecessary—surgeries. I will never know how much my desire to conform to men's sex-driven ideal damaged my body's health; I know only that it did, and that it was feminism that gave me the self-esteem and courage to reclaim and heal myself.

Despite the almost superwoman efforts of The Women's Movement, however, our hatred of our female bodies is even more evident now than ever before. "How do I hate thee, body dear? I cannot count the ways."

Notwithstanding the ubiquity and sheer numbers of these ways, for the most part they are taboo subjects for discussion outside of support groups. We insist that how we treat our bodies is no one's business but our own. What business is it of mine that my friend's lifestyle daily undermines her health and happiness? She is only hurting herself, after all.

But for women, who are connected to one another in deepest, most encompassing ways, hurting ourselves does hurt other women. John Donne had it backwards when he wrote that no man is an island; the fact is that every man is an island, disconnected from every other man and every other being. It is women who are not islands. It is femaleness everywhere that is an ineluctable unity of spirit that surpasses any bond possible for men to experience or even understand. My friend's refusal to care affectionately for herself hurts me, too, not just because I care about her, but because I *am* her.

So though she has an absolute right to live as she chooses in every way, and though out of respect the rest of us must keep silent, her choices do matter to all of us. When she damages her own health—by eating poorly, for example—she hurts all of us, depleting the energy not only of other women everywhere but of every female being: the polar bears, the oceans, the baby deer, the forests, rocks, and clouds, the great-hearted elephants. Since these are who we are, they are who we hurt when we hurt ourselves. When we punish ourselves for being female—as we have been profoundly conditioned to do—we also punish them.

How can we say we love women when we do not treat our own woman selves with loving kindness and mercy? If we are willing to do the most difficult form of activism—i.e., if we resolve to act as if we love ourselves as females—we cannot avoid taking into account our physical health; it is indivisible from our spiritual and emotional health and from the beings we most genuinely are.

Women's relationships with our bodies, and particularly with food, are one of the most highly charged of our "issues." Innumerable books have been written, workshops and conferences held, on this subject. So though we've heard lots of psychobabble, we also have a glimmer here and there of genuine understanding. We have friends who have confided the anguish they suffer from food addictions of one variety or another; who inform us that these are the most difficult of all addictions to conquer, and are rampant—almost endemic— among women at this stage of patriarchy.

We watch our friends eating carelessly—often downright dangerously—and almost have to put a sock in our mouths to keep from giving them unsolicited (i.e., matronizing) advice. But most of us have had to learn to avoid discussing anything related to food even with our best friends. The subject is too fraught with irresolvable conflict and sadomasochism, surrounded by too much tension and anger.

This does not mean we need to find better ways of discussing it, or of trying to persuade any woman to change her food-related behavior. Unless she asks for it, she neither wants our advice nor would—or could—take it if we gave it. We have no choice but to honor her wishes, stated or made clear in other ways. What the tension and anger around this subject prove is how very important it is to each of us to eat and otherwise do our lives as we choose without judgment or hassle from others.

All we can do, therefore—and this is hard enough—is monitor *ourselves*, take seriously our absolutely non-trivial obligation to our own bodies. The beginning of acting as if we love ourselves is to take dedicated stewardship of our personal health. Even if we can change our habits in only the smallest, simplest ways at first—or at long last—any evidence of our loving intent toward our bodies will generate powerful physical energy in and all around us, enough for us and for the planet and other females to share, with lots left over.

If we care enough, we can do a little research and even have the humility to experiment with eating in ways we once may have scorned or ridiculed. For the sake of all we value, all we most deeply desire, we need to consider adopting any diet that has the merit of being more healthful than the average American diet, more able to generate the female energy we so desperately need.

If we say we love women and the earth, we need to demonstrate that love; as the cliché has it, we need to walk the walk, not just talk the talk. If we are honest about our desire to be activists in saving the planet and all female life, we must begin by being honest first about saving our own lives. The way we treat our bodies—the study, the effort we put into acting as if we honor them—this is the surest measure of our love for ourselves, for the planet, and for femaleness everywhere.

To the extent that we can act as if we love our bodies, we create the essential and unique physical power we are here on the planet now to share with Earth's body. Until we take our own bodies seriously, we cannot truthfully say we care about hers or anyone else's, and we will be unable to help as we otherwise could when we are most needed.

If we honestly care—or even *want* to care—about Planet Earth and females everywhere, if we genuinely want a new world, none of this seems too much to ask of ourselves or one another—or for Earth herself to ask of us . . . does it?

Many of us say that we are gravely affected by watching Earth's agonizing decline at men's hands. We say it is as if we ourselves are dying. We say we would do anything to stop it. But how far does "anything" mean we are prepared to go?

Very far, I hope, demonstrating our love for femaleness from now all the way to the end of patriarchy as if the whole world and all our lives depended on it.

Because they do.

Chapter 17

The Sisterhood of the Spirit

We never intended to face this tumultuous time alone. All along we've known that surviving the end of patriarchy and the re-emergence of our world would require an immense fusion of female energy. So here we are, having promised in many lives between the Burning Times and the present day to gather this power by gathering ourselves together in unity—often, and on any pretext.

Already we are in great need of courage in our lives. In their desperate struggle to survive against immense odds, males are sucking all the oxygen out of our lungs and marrow out of our bones, leaving us with less and less physical and emotional energy and more and more need for them.

But almost worse is the effect upon our spirits. These times are eroding our hope and laying siege to our belief in ourselves as a community of power. In truth, the current situation presents us with a problem we didn't anticipate even when we were imagining the worst: this is very likely the most difficult possible time ever to try to rouse ourselves to get women together, even just to believe in the necessity for it.

For protection against rampaging disorder, we have retreated into our personal lives, managing just enough interest and will to deal adequately with the business of daily life. When our stress levels are already sky high, it is hard to care about future possibilities, and about such abstractions as raising female energy to save ourselves and our planet.

But somehow, try as we might to dismiss our inner voices and persuade ourselves that everything is just going to go along as it always has, somehow we can't turn away. After all, many of us have been activists most of our adult lives. We've been activists because something inside us insists that we are here at this time for a purpose. That knowledge won't let us rest.

So we keep on trying to find one another, to establish a group of women friends; because for the job we came to do we need to access our original female power—even if only a smidgen of it—and this takes more courage than we can generate alone. In fear of men's reprisals, we have hidden our power deeply away inside ourselves—and from ourselves as well as from them. Even those of us who know we have it somewhere are afraid of believing in it, to say nothing of re-membering how to find it. This is why we need one another.

To come together with other like-hearted women as often as possible—this is our most certain road back into memories of our amazing selves. Even if our group is small, just three or four, it is still our surest source of hope, courage, and safety; and also of faith enough in ourselves to be useful now to our universal female community.

Depending upon the degree to which we are willing to act as if we love and respect femaleness, any time we are with other women we re-establish the unseen spiritual community that defines us as females. Our profound connection to all things female is the greatest attribute of our species and the foundation of our power. This is why when we are with other women we can come nearer to our power than we ever can alone; and why the more of us there are—preferably in one place, but at least recognizing ourselves as part of one great spiritual Sisterhood—the more courage and energy we have to do this.

For the present, let's pretend we have been taking seriously the imperative to gather, and that we are now part of a group whose participants have agreed to meet regularly to embolden one another and to think together about surviving the chaos and dangers of the end of patriarchy. Where can we begin?

Why not begin with fun? Monique Wittig reminds us that once we walked safely everywhere "full of laughter." What a picture of contentment and freedom this conjures up! And what a place to start—being full of laughter. There is no reason we can't be full of laughter right now, and by laughing robustly at least once a day, alone or with others, there is no reason we can't help heal women's souls and bodies, and even prevent further suffering. It has the added advantage of being a pleasurable and easy way to create energy among us.

For instance, alone (or together) in our showers and bathtubs, with friends at dinner or parties or meetings we can all agree simply to begin to laugh—whether we are amused or not. Laughter works even without humor, though it is so contagious that we will soon be amused just by hearing ourselves laughing.

Why not try it right now? Simply begin to laugh and see how long you can keep it going. I have found that laughing loudly helps me continue. (Pause here for laughter.) Now, the next time you're showering, or getting dressed, or making dinner—whatever is the best time for you to remember to do this every day—you can laugh again, a little longer each time. Even if you feel foolish, soon you'll be able to laugh for a full minute—even though it may seem interminable; then five minutes, and finally fifteen minutes, anywhere, anytime—and you won't care a fig when your next-door neighbors eye you warily.

Fifteen minutes of laughter a day is a source of free insurance against depression and physical illness. The rhythmic spasms of laughter—very like the spasms of orgasm—gently massage and exercise our organs and glands, increasing their morale, efficiency, and health. As we gulp air into our lungs, our hearts pump extra-oxygen-rich blood through every cell. Our brains glow with energy. Every atom of us relaxes with well-being. While we laugh—and for some time afterward—despair loses its hold on our psyches, and we are glad to be alive.

If laughing without being amused seems too silly at first, we can concentrate on finding funny things to read together and comedies to watch; we can dress in costumes and dance or do improvisational plays, or both. We can play active, participatory parlor games of all sorts—we are often at our wittiest in these. We can even have a short joke-telling prelude to otherwise sedate meetings. When we read or hear or think of something laughable, we can share it again and again, generating positive healing energy all over the place. Laughter also unifies, and since women unified are dangerous to the status quo, the energy we generate from laughing together is of a wondrously subversive variety.

Recently, I read some bloopers from newspaper headlines and church bulletins that were so funny I've kept them on the refrigerator door. Following my own advice to share, I'm including a few of them here:

Something went wrong in jet crash, experts say.

Miners refuse to work after death.

Include your children when baking cookies.

Witnesses state that the plane 'was very close to the ground when it crashed.'

For those of you who have children and don't know it, we have a nursery downstairs.

Please place your donation in the envelope along with the deceased person you want remembered.

The ladies of the church have cast off clothing of every kind.

They may be seen in the basement on Friday afternoon.

Low Self Esteem Support Group will meet Thursday at 7 p.m. Please use back door.

Bilingual chicken dinner this Sunday at noon.

(bumper sticker) Witches parking only. All others will be toad.

So we laugh together, and calling to mind later what we laughed about allows us to laugh about it all over again as well as to re-experience the relaxation and fun we felt the first time. A little fit of laughter can be made to go a long way.

As another method of increasing energy and hope in our own lives as well as universally, our group of women decides to try to follow Wittig's injunction to remember and invent our female selves.

So maybe while we are all still mellow from a bout of hilarity, we sit down to a meal together. One woman among us, however, is so eager to "make an effort to remember, or failing that, invent," so eager to feel her power, not just hypothesize about it, that she finishes quickly, and as we begin our dessert, informs us that she wants to make up a story about herself on the spot and tell it to us as if it were true. She assures us that in essence it *will* be true because she cannot possibly overstate her case, in patriarchy can never imagine herself even partially as powerful and magnificent as she truly is.

Soon, when we are all settled comfortably and ready to listen, she closes her eyes and begins:

"The night is too beautiful for sleep, so I decide to go for a walk in the big field out behind my house. As I start down the path, I feel a coyote muzzle brush my hand; I reach down and stroke her head and she licks me. Up above us a great barn owl makes a U-turn to check us out before swooping down and settling softly on my shoulder. She folds her wings, I put my arm around her, lay my cheek against her downy body, and she gives me a little peck on the eyebrow.

"As the three of us continue out into the field, the bears join us and the deer, bobcats, rabbits, nighthawks and magpies, the horses and raccoons and snakes—all moving and talking together softly through the dark, side by side.

"We head for the enormous old cottonwood tree down at the end of the field, walking gradually up through the air so that by the time we reach her we're standing in the starry darkness above her topmost branches. We sit down in her aura, feeling her energy surge up around us, into, and through us, feel the power of her glad heart, her hope, her pleasure in our company. Sitting here in the air, we lick and nuzzle each other—the fur, the feathers, the skin, the scales, the feelers.

"Purring, hissing, howling, we are having a fine time up here together when suddenly—a premonition! Ears, heads, tails fly up, and we leap to our feet as—look!—the moon clears the rim of the mountain and rises into the sky, an enormous soaring world. Before we can even say Aaaah! we are up there with her among the stars, and the moon is us and we are the moon, and the stars are us and we are the stars—all one consciousness, one great love, in this park between the worlds.

"Looking about ourselves in this endless starry space, we see women and other beings from other planets, other universes, animals, insects, birds, and fish the likes of which we had forgotten existed. And from our home planet, the dogs and elephants and spiders—everybody is up here tonight in the moonlight. It's so amazing, so marvelous, we can hardly take it in! We don't even have to talk because, being one another, we know exactly what everyone is feeling, what everyone is about. In this intimacy, we overflow with happiness.

"Our arms around one another, our hands touching faces—it's been too long since we've been together like this. As I stroke the tough skin of my elephant sister lying next to me in the air, I 'talk' with her in the same way that everyone is 'talking' in this circle—heart-to-heart, life-to-life, not bound and gagged by language or species differences.

"On my other side, an Arcturan woman takes my hand, and I am wonderstruck that we too speak the same language—the language of being female, of truly knowing each other. What she feels, I feel; who I am, she experiences as if she were me. Only by being one another are we finally and fully being ourselves.

"As the moon moves toward morning, we part at last, but not before we promise to come together again soon in this cosmic amphitheater that unites our worlds.

"Then once again I find myself by the bend of the river above the old cottonwood, watching my companions of this night disperse silently down the air into the moonlit hills and fields of planet Earth."

The storyteller stops, looks around the table at her friends' faces, her own face soft and warm with a dream from which she has not yet quite wakened. "Yes," she says quietly, "that's what I did last night."

The woman at her side squeezes her hand, then tells us that she also has a story for us. (From "Remembering" by jody jew-dyke, first printed in Sinister Wisdom, the "Lesbian Utopia" issue, Fall 2007. Excerpted here with jody's permission.)

"One day, so very long ago, I awoke and something had happened. I heard the birds outside my window and for the first time Heard them. In my Mind. I Heard them laughing and cheering and saying, its OK Now. The Earth is Ours again. I wasn't sure if I was quite awake, though I Knew this was Real. As I lay in my soft bed, Listening, an Excitement welling up inside of me, the Feline companion who had been sharing her Life with me, and was curled in a soft ball by my head, also Awoke. She looked at me, slowly stretched and Smiled. She too laughed and said its OK Now, Oh Purrrrr,

Finally the Earth is Ours again. They are gone and will never return. We will never know fear again. Oh Purrrrr.

"I was filled with an overwhelming sense of Joy, as tears ran down my face and could not move as I tried to take it all in. Looked into her eyes and Listened. I Heard more. I heard the trees laughing. I heard the plants laughing. I heard the seeds and the worms and the tiny flying ones, the water, the rocks, the soil, all cheering. The excitement flooded into me and I leapt up to run outside and could Feel it. I Knew it had finally happened.

"The males were gone. And so was every harmful thing they had brought with them. They and their destructiveness were gone. Completely, without a trace.

"I thought of my Friends and immediately Heard them cheering, saying, Yes, I Know. How Amazing! OH YES, We are Free. Its Over. No, its just Begun. Yes, YES. And then All those I Knew and those I as yet did not know, in All the many languages started coming through. And we were all laughing and crying and shouting with glee and dancing and hugging and kissing and rolling in the grasses, and frolicking in the snow, and caressing the flowers and hugging the trees and splashing in the waters. We were All Connected and we All Knew.

"And so it Began.

"It took so much less time than you would think to Become Fully OurSelves again. . . .It was remarkable how quickly we moved past and healed the pain and damage. It was amazing how quickly we shed the fear and mistrust. It was wonderful how quickly our bodies, minds and spirits healed and renewed and opened. The Knowing of our Connectedness, the Hearing of All just catapulted us into this fine World as we Know it Now.

"Faster than we could sing 'ding dong heteropatriarchy's gone', we were All living in the world of Our Dreams."

Her neighbor at the table urges her, "Go on! Please, go on."
"No," she answers, "it's your turn now."

Her neighbor thinks for a moment, and says, "Well, I don't
have such a fine story, but I can tell you that this is what I
remember: my wings catching the updraft and slowly spiral-
ing me up through the clouds. The wind streaming through
my feathers, and my whole soul rejoicing." She looks eagerly
around the table. "Do you remember that? The freedom of flying? Do you dream about it?"

We assure her that we do remember, and talk together
awhile about dreams of flying. Then another woman says she
has a true story to tell, and we quiet down to listen.

"I was at work one afternoon when suddenly I felt something distinctly un-human though somehow familiar happening to my hands. Looking down at them lying on my desk, I
saw—instead of my woman's small, domesticated hands—the
huge, feral paws of a tiger. I realized at once that what I was
feeling in my hands was me retracting my claws."

Across the table, a woman leans forward in excitement.
"Hey, I've had that feeling! I've never mentioned it or heard
anyone else talk about it, though. Wow! I've got goose-bumps!"

We laugh and clap, aroused by her enthusiasm, and the
tiger woman stands and takes a wry bow.

Returning from the stove with a hot cup of tea, another
of us sits back down at the table, and says, "I had a similar
experience once, except that when it happened I was sitting in
the dentist's waiting room leafing through a tattered copy of
'People.' Suddenly, I began to feel myself expand as if I were a
balloon, my body getting tighter and tighter, fuller and fuller,
and I noticed—it seemed completely natural at the time—
that the room around me had become a meadow.

"So, there, to the accompaniment of bees buzzing and
larks singing, I relived being a milkweed with a very pregnant

seedpod. A long dreamy and indescribably sensual afternoon went by in a few minutes as I grew huger and huger, until suddenly my pod burst open and out into the sunshine flew thousands of downy little parachutes! Aaaaaaah! Better than orgasm."

Everyone cheers and claps, and someone asks, "In what way 'better than orgasm'?

"Total bodied!" the pod-woman answers promptly.

Then we say to one another, "We really could experience such things, couldn't we. We lived such lives, were really once this multi-dimensional kind of being."

Those who didn't tell a story about themselves agree to have one ready for us the next time we get together. Then, as time passes and at each gathering we hear more tales they become wilder and more astonishing. We discover that every time we think and talk about the immensity of our power, we feel our spirits expand and our possibilities stretch out farther before us. We get more and stronger glimmerings of ourselves as unlimited possibility, ready now—like ripe milkweed seedpods—to burst open and fill the universe.

In addition, every time we come together as a group, we spend some time brainstorming for more ways to change our feelings about ourselves, more ways to continue to increase our female love-and-respect quotient, to up the odds of accessing some of our original power. We have ideas about how to strengthen our own and our planet's immune systems. Maybe nothing original or world-shaking, but places to begin.

For instance, we decide that it's time for all of us, but particularly those of us who habitually speak too softly, to stop mumbling. It's time to overcome our socialization to be genteel and demure and, instead, to undermine men's psychic hold on us by making big noises—drumming, roaring, honking, bellowing, howling, barking, hee-hawing. We decide to over-come our socialization to be "ladies."

In fact, not only do we adamantly refuse to be ladies, but we also refuse to use the word "lady" to refer to any woman—not so much for her sake as for our own: to keep our awareness sharp, to act and feel respectful of women. As Ella Wheeler Wilcox, American poet, journalist, and free thinker, once wrote:

"Give us that grand word 'woman' once again, and let's have done with 'lady'; one's a term full of fine force, strong, beauti-ful and firm, fit for the noblest use of tongue or pen; and one's a word for lackeys." (Ella Wheeler Wilcox lived from 1850 to 1919. Some of her most famous quotes are available on the Internet from Jone Johnson Lewis, 1997-2004, "Ella Wheeler Wilcox Quotations," About Women's History, http://womenshistory.abhout.com/library/bio/biwilcox.htm, October 31, 2009.)

While this distinction between "woman" and "lady" is val-id and useful, the truth is that the word "woman" does not describe us accurately either, no matter how many variations of spelling we use to try to make it right. Women, wimmin, womyn—nothing of what we are coincides even vaguely with either the denotation or the connotation of any spelling, or of any spelling of any word for us in any language. So I simply live with the word "woman" as I live with the wrongness of all language.

I feel pretty much the same way about "girl" as I do about "lady," only not quite so strongly. Nowadays, it's chic, when speaking humorously or lightly, to refer to one's good friends as "girl"—as in, "You go, girl!"

Perhaps I'm just an old fuddy-duddy, but I don't want to be called "girl" any more than I want to be called "lady." If "you go, woman!" is too stuffy, everyone who wants to encourage me to "go" is invited to say instead, "You go, old bat!" "You go, hag!" "You go, you old witch!" Or as a last resort, "You go, Sonia!" I am not a girl, but I am an old bat, a hag, a crone, and Sonia. Perhaps also an old fuddy-duddy—if so, then, "You go, you old fuddy-duddy!" will do.

Since we are stuck with language for the time being, we can use it for our own ends; for instance, to come closer to our power by clarifying and rejecting some of the obvious ways we abet misogyny.

The word "vagina," for instance. This very personal and totally female word is almost always misused in patriarchy. Because it is an organ of obsessive interest to men, in most of their minds it reigns alone and supreme between our legs.

Though women know better, at least in our spoken language we often follow their unfortunate example and use "vagina" to designate the entire vulva. In fact, many women do not even know the word "vulva"—and if they do, are often not sure what it includes, or how to use the term correctly.

My own ignorance was witnessed by hundreds of women over many years. Back in my speech-making days, I would come out onto the stage holding both my hands high in the vee symbol. When I reached the microphone, I would wave the vee's and call out to the audience, "Do you know what this is?" After a weak response of "Peace? Victory?" I would shout: "Vagina Power"! And all the dykes and would-be dykes in the audience would stomp and clap and whistle.

But when the speaking part of my career was almost at an end, Harriet Lerner came to talk at the university in Albuquerque and stayed overnight in our home. In the course of our conversations, she told me kindly—and too late—that what I had really meant to shout all those years was "Vulva Power!" I knew at once—to my embarrassment—that she was right. Much later, when I attended a performance of "The

Vagina Monologues," I remembered that night with Harriet and thought that their author also probably meant "The Vulva Monologues." Probably she, too, learned too late of her mistake.

Using the inclusive term "vulva" helps deprogram us from the belief that the only significant thing "down there" is the vagina, the receptacle for men's penises and the escape route for their progeny—the only useful "thing."

Earlier, I mentioned sharing incidents we find funny. When I wrote "down there" just now I was reminded of a joke I heard years ago from Sequoia Edwards of Albuquerque: a mother told her young daughter, who was stepping into the shower, never to wash herself "down there." So for more than a year the girl didn't wash her feet.

Harking back to an earlier chapter, another power-awakening deprogramming exercise is to replace the phrase "the men in power" with "the men in weakness," or "the men in control" and when speaking of women, whenever possible to say, "the women in power." I can personally vouch for this as a very strong deprogramming tool; after all these years, the treason of it still shakes me awake every time I do it.

Another commandment to get into the habit of breaking is, instead of using the pronouns "he" and "him," using "she" and "her" whenever gender is in doubt. "Look at the bird in the feeder; isn't she beautiful!" Or, "Is she a stray cat?" Or, "What an interesting dog; what breed is she?" Or, "You have a baby chick! What's her name?"

When I catch sight of a deer as I walk in the forest, for example, I deliberately think and speak of it as female, as in "Look at her! Do you see her? She seems very young." Evidence of the strong deprogramming value of doing this is the response of acquaintances who, when I break this particular commandment in their presence, almost always demand testily, "How do you know it's female?" To which I retort testily, "How do you know she's *not*?"

Their discomfort is simply more evidence that because programming always sounds right, deprogramming always sounds wrong (and makes us cross). Thinking of and calling everything male until proven otherwise is so deeply ingrained in us that consciously to turn it around is heretical, and like all heresy, supremely satisfying to the soul. Every time I say "she" when my enculturation commands me to say "he" until I find out otherwise (and sometimes persevering even then), I feel a fine jolt of power rush across my dissident tongue and flood my rebellious heart.

Because disobeying even men's minor edicts takes aware-ness and courage, doing it strengthens our respect for our-selves, revealing us to ourselves as the strong, intelligent, brave beings we are, reminding us cogently that we are not total slaves. This opens the way for more truth and freedom to re-verberate through our daily lives.

Something else we decide during our brainstorming ses-sions is that one way to honor and show respect for other women is to refrain from giving them unsolicited advice and opinion. If a woman tells us she is having financial difficulty, for example, unless she asks for our help, we matronize her by giving her advice about her money situation. If a woman has an illness, it is condescending as well as none of our busi-ness, to "teach" her how to take better care of herself. When a woman's relation-ship is floundering in turbulent seas, un-less she specifically requests our navigational assistance, we belittle her by explaining how she and her partner can sail on with greater ease. Unsolicited advice and opinion is always disrespectful. A friend who will listen is all most of us need or want—unless we say otherwise.

Just a few words about ageism and condescension in general. Like most of us, but particularly middle-aged and old women, I feel unbearably patronized when called "young lady" by unctuous shopkeepers—usually male—as in, "What can I do for you, young lady?" But men are not the only offenders. I feel the same way when I reveal my age or refer to myself as an old woman and other women protest, "Oh, you're not old!" or "Just think of yourself as 74 years young!" or "You're only as old as you feel!" and other anti-old clichés.

If at 74 I am not yet old enough to be referred to as "old," how old do I have to be before I am old enough? The fact is, I am not 74 years old because I think or feel or act a certain way but because I have lived for 74 years. To insinuate otherwise is blatantly ageist. When have we ever heard someone say she is 45 years old and been rebutted with, "No, you're not; you're 45 years young!"

So far as I'm concerned, 74 is old, no matter how strong, healthy, and energetic I am, and there is nothing wrong with that. Being an old woman is not inherently bad, except perhaps in the eyes of men—and, alas, also some women—who find it sexually disgusting. But who cares about them?

In fact, I find not being initially and primarily assessed as a prospective sex partner one of the most liberating aspects of being old. Now because of our advanced age, friends and I can see more clearly how darling we are in a myriad of important ways other than sexual.

The ageism and sexism of the term "dear," usually offends me, too. It is directed primarily to women, children, and old people, and reveals the sort of ersatz closeness one feels toward lesser beings.

I witnessed how demeaning and inappropriate the word "dear" can be when years ago my daughter, Kari, had a "dear" experience (with ageism thrown in for good measure). I had been invited to speak at an ERA fund-raising event given by and for Hollywood notables—actors (both female and male), directors, playwrights, and so on. Kari accompanied me. At the reception after the event, a very famous, essentially kind and well-meaning woman approached our group and asked Kari, "How old are you, dear?" Kari answered, "I'm 16, dear. How old are you?"

Just as "old" does not necessarily mean in one's dotage, demented, helpless, or ill, neither does it necessarily mean "wiser," "kinder," or "more understanding." It means simply that one has lived a certain large number of years, has perhaps learned something from this, but then again often has not; perhaps has been refined and expanded by life, but on the other hand, may have been coarsened, diminished, or embittered by it. An old woman is not automatically more spiritually enlightened than a younger one. To assume sage-like wisdom in an old woman is just as ageist as to assume stupidity.

In our brainstorming sessions, we talk a great deal about women's health. We decide that now, in this critical time when we most need to live through the end of mensworld and on into our own, we must try to remember how to make and keep the planet and all female life healthy. Since this is well within our capabilities, it requires only our belief and determination.

When the mormon church was first organized, the teaching was that every member could lay their hands on the sick and heal them. (Of course, since they were doing it in the context of a christian religion, they had first to invoke Jesus' power in order to believe they could do it; heaven forefend that they should think they had such powers in themselves!) However, though both women and men went around purporting to heal, women had by far the better success record.

What happened next was inevitable. The men whined about the women to god and god in his heaven promptly commanded the mormon "prophet" not to allow women to heal in the name of deity; clearly this privilege and power was reserved for men, god's fraternity brothers.

So for almost two hundred years, mormon women have believed they can't heal, and the most unenlightened, obtuse, oafs of men believe they can. But I can attest to the truth that anytime anyone is healed by men's "laying on of hands," it is because some woman is sending her love and hope and—often without even meaning to—her healing power to that person.

Mormon women are not the only women who believe they can't heal, of course. Most of us believe we can't, either. We think we have to take workshops and learn "methods" from "healers" (often males) and perhaps pay considerable fees to do so—which alone should shout "fraud!"—when the truth is that femaleness, the power that keeps the planets spinning in their orbits, is the only healing power in the universe, and that women need understand nothing more than that.

I say that all we need to do is believe it. This is easier when we see it with our own eyes, or experience it in our own lives, as many of us have, and as I did a few years ago.

In excruciating pain, I was rushed to the hospital by ambulance late one night, lights flashing, sirens screaming. On the way, the EMTs monitoring my vital signs began to fear I was dying and wouldn't make it to the ER. So they asked Jade, "Are you going to be all right if we lose her?" Though I was still alive when we arrived at the hospital, no one in the ER could figure out how I'd lived to get there or what was the matter with me. Right away they ruled out appendicitis, since I was 71 years old, far too old to have appendicitis.

So while scans and tests of various sorts were sent to be read by specialists in other parts of the country, where someone finally figured out that 71 wasn't too old for appendicitis and that my appendix had to come out in the next 15 minutes or *else*—Jade and Braden, another woman friend, stood by the gurney and stroked my hair and face, arms, legs, and feet. For five hours they caressed me and kept that burgeoning appendix from bursting. I could feel their healing power radiating from their hands through my entire body. I know that my friends' female power not only kept my appendix quiet and soothed, but maintained all the rest of my body in perfect health through it all.

My women friends saved my life. There is no doubt in either my mind or anybody else's who was there that night that without them I would have died. The nurses knew it; they could hardly believe I survived. But I not only survived: I felt well and vigorous, up, trailing my I.V. equipment through the halls the next day, demanding to go home.

Enough of us have experienced or witnessed miraculous recoveries at women's hands that we know our healing power is real. We need now to raise that power, not only to heal Earth but to heal ourselves and one another, to banish the diseases patriarchy has specially designed for women that are stealing so much of our energy and happiness. We can do this easily—or could if we were in our right minds.

Together we can help one another get closer to our right minds, to learn to respect ourselves and other females enough to get this power back. Together we are less afraid to take seriously that this is what we promised to do—to return at this time and grow into our powerful female selves, become bigger than we ever dreamed possible, be the women who can save one another's lives and all beneficent life, who can save this planet.

Together we can begin right now to *be* the new female world—each of us figuring out how to do this in the context of our own lives. All we can expect of ourselves is that we make our best stab at it.

As I have already written repeatedly, to be of any use at all when we are most needed at this critical time, we need—if at all possible—to survive physically the interim between now and the end of maleness, the period Jade and I refer to as the HTA: the Hard Times Ahead. What I haven't gone into at all, and will only mention in passing, are the preparations we will have to make in order to stay alive as men's systems function more and more sporadically and ultimately break down forever. Despite the fear that prevents many of us from even thinking about this and perhaps makes us pooh-pooh the whole notion, if we mean to keep our covenant with Earth and one another, we have to consider it a possibility and act accordingly.

We can do this much more easily if we do it together. Women together automatically generate bravery, more than enough of it to face preparing to have no electricity for heat, light, water, and communication, no gasoline for transportation, no propane for cooking and heating, and no food or medicine except what we have put away for such an eventuality. The internet is full of help for those whose intuition is telling them that everything we take for granted is becoming more and more ephemeral.

Many folks are very afraid, so afraid they cannot bear to look at what they would have to do if they faced that fear; I meet them almost every day now—the roofing guy, for instance, who confided to me yesterday that he has taken up smoking again after five years of abstinence because he's so afraid his whole industry is coming down.

He didn't mention doing anything to make sure he and his family would be ready if this happens; instead, he smokes. Others drink, or eat too much, or shop, or watch untold hours of television, or read until their eyes ache—whatever it is that dulls their anxiety; everything but face the possibility and do what will really allay their fear: get busy getting ready. Just in case.

I'll never forget the first time someone besides my closest friends spoke to me about this. I had been thinking for a dozen years or more about the eventuality of all men's systems falling apart when one day I was third in line at a supermarket in Tucson. Just as the first in line was taking out his credit card to pay, the woman who was second in line turned to me and announced, "This just can't go on!"

I couldn't figure out what her problem was; her turn was obviously just five seconds away. Seeing my confusion, she tried again: "*The world* cannot go on this way!"

"I couldn't agree more!" I said to her back as, having made her pronouncement and got it off her chest, she turned around to attend to the business of paying.

A group of us here are working together to make sure we can sustain ourselves—that we have access to water, food, heat, and shelter for one to five years. We're collecting rainwater, planting gardens, using homemade composting toilets, canning. The more we talk about it and the more we actually prepare, the less frightening the possibility seems of being without patriarchy's superstructure. Hoping passionately that I will live into the HTA and beyond in my beloved body, I personally am determined to do all I know how to do—physically, emotionally, and spiritually—to be ready.

I love my preparations; they give substance to my hope.

My hope is that you, too, will survive and that you'll be alive somewhere on this planet with us when one fine day maleness disappears forever and once again all is female.

❧ ❧ ❧

Chapter 18

The Embrace

I haven't forgotten the women on the hillside in Wheathampstead in that terrible last year of the 16th century, those terrible last few days of their lives. The rest of that story is short and I will tell you what I know of it.

But before I do, I must remind you that it is not the end of the story; no, not at all. Their real story, like ours—the story that has been waiting inside them for centuries, waiting through other lives, waiting for this time—is only just beginning. Like us, they live today somewhere on this planet, either in the flesh or in the spirit, as do the women the world over who promised in those days to be here with us now.

The friends we loved then and whose hands we held, whose tears mingled with ours, whose wet cheeks we kissed, then kissed again, in farewell—those steadfast and loving women are not far away from us even now as I write, even now as you read. If we sense that we have known some of our current friends or acquaintances forever, we are probably right.

When we sense that our friends in the spirit are near us, we are also undoubtedly right; all the women in the women-only spirit realms of every planet are now busy on those planets loving, helping, and encouraging us, their embodied sisters. We have never been alone, are not alone now, those of us who love femaleness truly and forever; alone neither in our beliefs nor in our undertakings.

As we know, however, our spirit friends cannot do for us what we can do for ourselves. Though with their broader knowledge and understanding of events and energies, they are often able to influence where we cannot, they are neither magicians nor gods. Still bound by the male paradigm, they are patriarchal women like us, not able to predict the timing of events with much greater accuracy than we can ourselves, and needing our energy, too, as we need theirs. But they lift our hearts and smooth the path for us in a myriad ways we cannot even begin to imagine.

We are peers, we embodied and non-embodied women, all of us in this together, all of us equally dependent on one another. And we are not an exclusive club. Any woman anywhere who cares about women and other female beings above all else is automatically one of us.

Now, the Englishwomen on the dark hillside.

When each group has finished in their small circles, they rise and join the others. Silently they walk into one another's open arms.

But they do not hug; they *embrace.*

An embrace is a testament to women's unsurpassable beauty, a whole-woman kiss and vow of faithfulness. It is an eloquent tribute to female power, and a solemn promise—a pact between and among us—that femaleness has all our loyalty forever. Embracing, these women encompass one another, welcome one another into their hearts and lives as part of themselves. Forever equals. Forever sisters. Forever lovers.

So there on that portentous night, the women of Wheathampstead embrace. Then, standing in a circle, their arms around one another, holding close and dear, they sing softly the songs that have been passed down as part of their oral memory-keeping through all the long lonely centuries of patriarchy. That we still sing a few of these songs, after thousands of years of suppression of female power, testifies to the fierceness and courage of our never-extinguished—our *non-extinguishable*—SisterWitch conspiracy.

The first chant-song, so ancient and still so familiar to us, seems created to remind us of knowledge about ourselves that men were steadily and systematically erasing. It continues to fulfill this mission:

Woman am I
Spirit am I
I am the infinite within myself.
I can find no beginning
I can find no end
All things I am

Remember this one? It is another chant-song that surely SisterWitches somewhere—during the massacres of women we call the Burning Times—sang to one another as they parted for the last time:

Listen, listen, listen to my heart's song;
Listen, listen, listen to my heart's song:
I will never forget thee, I will never forsake thee
I will never forget thee, I will never forsake thee.
Listen, listen, listen to my heart's song, etc.

And then there's a relatively new chant-like song that was brought to my attention only a few years ago, one that originated with the Wheathampstead covens:

I will always, always love thee;
I will never, never leave thee.
Take my hand, we'll dance together.
If you take my hand, we'll dance forever.
I will always, always love thee, etc.

I make up additional lyrics and verses to these and other melodies as I walk the forest paths of this place. I sing them all to you.

Now in the beautiful spring of 2010, I embrace you, my beloved SisterWitches both of the past and the present. With this embrace, I renew my ancient covenant to do and be whatever is necessary to reunite with you, wild and free once more, in the perfect power and intimacy of our female world.

Until then, and forever after, my dearest loves, you have my heart and my life.

About the Author

Although she received her doctorate from Rutgers in 1965, Sonia Johnson is prouder of her 1979 graduation *summa cum laude* from the Mormon church, the world's foremost university for patriarchal studies.

Catapulted overnight into national prominence by the excommunication, she became a Radical Feminist—and later a Lesbian—agitating, writing, and organizing for women's rights. In 1984 she campaigned as a feminist on three alternative party tickets for president of the United States, becoming the first candidate in U.S. history other than a Republican or Democrat to win matching funds from the federal government. For almost two decades she supported herself and her children with sales from her books and by speaking for universities, conferences, and organizations of all varieties.

The author of five previous books and still a passionate feminist, she lives with her partner of 19 years and three female animal friends in a community of women.

❦ ❦ ❦

Sonia Johnson may be reached for purchase of this book and for other inquiries at www.sonia-johnson.com or soniajohnson3@gmail.com

5475961R0

Made in the USA
Charleston, SC
20 June 2010